The Dead Rabbit
PADDY DRINKS
MODERN IRISH
WHISKEY COCKTAILS
The Dead Rabbit
IRISH WHISKEY

marinerbooks.com

Photograph on page 15: Doron Guild
Image on page 18: Kate and Tim Tomkinson
Photograph on page 28: Elaine Hill
Flavor Wheel Graphics: Marcus Lynam
Cover graphic: Mícheál Douglas
Concrete texture © Shutterstock: Sathaporn
Book design by Laurence Smith / Drinksology

Library of Congress Cataloging-in-Publication Data has been applied for.

ISBN 978-0-358-51286-8 (hbk)
ISBN 978-0-358-51290-5 (ebk)

Printed in the United States of America

1 2022

4500843875

PADDY DRINKS

MODERN IRISH WHISKEY COCKTAILS

—

JILLIAN VOSE, JACK MCGARRY & SEAN MULDOON
with CONOR KELLY

MARINER BOOKS

Boston   New York

CONTENTS

The Dead Rabbit
Grocery and Grog

WELCOME HOME

30

THE SONS AND DAUGHTERS OF ERIN AND THE AMERICAN BAR

by David Wondrich

Like every American art—movies, comic books, jazz—the art of the bar, with its lengthy roster of delightful iced drinks mixed to order, was built on the fly from whatever bricks were handy, without too much attention to where they came from. That can make it rather difficult to figure out exactly how the thing was built and who supplied each brick. But if you look closely enough at the American bar (as the rest of the world called it—we just called it the bar), you can see that a significant number of the bricks are stamped with the Irish harp.

When we think of the Irish influence on American drinking, we tend to think of bars such as McSorley's in New York, the Irish Bank in San Francisco, or the Brendan Behan Pub in Boston: down-to-earth joints that are a little piece of Ireland cut off from there and washed up here. While that level of dedication to authenticity might be exceptional, just about every town in America has at least one place that will serve you a pint of Guinness stout and a shot of Jameson in surroundings with a passing familiarity to the Emerald Isle—even if the rest of the taps yield Bud and Bud Light, the spirit most usually poured is Fireball, and they don't know their *céilí* from their *céad míle fáilte*. The "Irish" bar has become a part of American culture just like the "Italian" pizzeria.

But that's only the most visible part of the story. The Irish influence goes far beyond shamrocks and shillelaghs, affecting everything from the spirits we drink to what we chase them with, the cocktails we mix them into, and even the way we relate with our bartenders and each other when we're in the bar.

The first wave of Irish drink-slingers in America—if you can call a slow and intermittent trickle a "wave"—was made up of true pioneers, coming to a land where even the most rudimentary benchmarks of European civilization were still being built. We don't know much about them; often, there is only a name, a year, a place. We know that Thomas Innis (or Ennis) was granted a license in 1661 to keep an "ordinary"—basically, the colonial equivalent of a bar & grill—at Innis' Choice, the tract of land he owned in St. Mary's County, Maryland, and that he traded drinks for pounds of tobacco, the most common currency of that time and place. We can't even say for sure that he was Irish, since Innis can also be a Scottish name. O'Dwyer, however, not so much, and in 1687 one Edmund O'Dwyer was keeping an inn at Wye Town, across the Chesapeake in Talbot County. By then, Edward Mortimer, described as "an Irishman," had had a public house up in Boston for at least a decade.

The first Irish-run bar in New York that I've been able to locate came only in the 1720s, near the end of the first wave. It was also likely to have been New York's first cop bar. Dennis Mahany, its proprietor, held the unlovely post of public whipper, responsible for flogging the city's duly sentenced miscreants. I can't imagine that the patronage at his rum-punch house, in New York's rough-and-tumble West Ward, was overrefined in character.

We know so very little about these pioneers and the establishments they ran that it's difficult to evaluate their importance. But to be Irish and a tavern keeper in seventeenth- and early eighteenth-century America was to have at least one advantage that Englishmen lacked. The Irish were spirits drinkers (to be fair, so were the Scots). Until the notorious Gin Craze, which began among the lower classes in the 1710s, and the contemporaneous Punch Craze—which was upper class and hence politely ignored—the English barely touched the stuff. In the colonies, however, the climate made it hard to brew beer and the infrastructure made it even harder to transport it, while the phylloxera louse saw to it that all wine would have to be imported, and therefore expensive. To be a colonial was to be a spirits drinker.

That noted, based on the very limited information that has survived, there seems to have been little to distinguish these early Irish-owned bars from their non-Irish contemporaries. That would begin to change with the second wave of Irish tavern keepers, which came in the middle of the eighteenth century. This one was substantial. By the 1750s, for example, the list of New York's license holders included Doyles and Egans, Dolans and Rileys, Kellys, Lynches, and Kennedys, among many others, male and female (women tavern keepers were much more common in colonial times than after the Revolution). More importantly, publicans began to trade on their Hibernian origins: by 1758, Philadelphia could boast of both a Jolly Irishman tavern and a Faithful Irishman, while twenty years later, Martin Doyle went all out and called his place in New York the Faithful Irishman and Jolly Sailors.

By then, of course, the city was under occupation by the British Army, the colonies having decisively severed their political system from the mother country's. In the process, they also wrenched their culture off into new directions, affecting everything from the way they spelled their words to what they drank and where they drank it.

We can see that new world in a June 1820 advertisement in the *New York Evening Post* for Byrne's Fly-Market Hotel, where the proprietor boasts of his "Ice Punch." Iced drinks were at the cutting edge of American drinking: the creation in the opening decades of the nineteenth century of a system for the cheap and efficient distribution of ice in the summertime was one of the decisive factors in moving American drinking away from its European roots.

Murtagh Byrne, the hotel's proprietor, arrived from county Wicklow in 1817 and opened a grocery. After that burned down in 1819, he opened the hotel on what is now Maiden Lane. It was a respectable place, and he and his wife, Alicia, also from Ireland, put a great deal of effort into making the bar and dining room places where one could reliably expect to find the good things in this world. They were known for their turtle soup, their oysters, and their way with the other delicacies of the day; indeed, their sign bore a turtle and a partridge. They were also known for the "very superior old Irish whiskey" that they sold both by the barrel and by the drink. (Irish whiskey, which had undergone a rapid evolution at the end of the 1700s, began making its way to America in the 1790s.) In the winter, the bar would gladly make it into "Hot Punch," as Byrne advertised it. It's also quite possible that their summer "Ice Punch" was based on it as well, although in general, Irish whiskey punch—the progenitor of the "hot whiskey" still enjoyed throughout Ireland in the winter—was served hot.

Byrne's place was evidently a popular one, but unfortunately, he was carried off by the yellow fever epidemic of 1822. Alicia continued for a while without him, but then the Fly-Market Hotel disappears from the record. Still, it's interesting to think what might have been, had they survived; to visualize Byrnes' hotel acting like a sort of Irish Delmonico's, holding to the highest standards as it made the Irish case for culinary and mixological excellence. Even without a champion like Byrne, Irish whiskey punch was for a time in the 1830s and '40s a fashionable drink in the United States, to the point that in Washington, DC it was included in the short list of drinks whose prices were regulated by the local innkeepers' association.

But then Irish American drinking went a different way, at least for a while. Irish immigration had been growing steadily in the 1820s and '30s, bringing in mostly Protestants from Ulster. However, the failure of the Irish potato crop in 1845 and the ensuing Great Hunger turned that flow into a flood, with most of the literally millions who arrived in America coming from the island's Catholic south and west. In the cities they where they settled—New York, Boston, Philadelphia, New Orleans, and Chicago, but also smaller industrial towns throughout the Northeast and Midwest—the new arrivals reached enough of a critical mass to populate whole neighborhoods, complete with churches, groceries, and, of course, bars.

The new Irish bars were rarely anything fancy: most of the new immigrants came to the country with little more than the clothes on their backs. For the greater part, these establishments fell into the class of bar known at the time as a "shades." Unlike the straight-out American bar—where you went in, stood at the bar, tossed back your Improved Whiskey Cocktail or Brandy Straight, and sauntered out again—in a shades, you could sit a spell. In an 1865 article, the *Brooklyn Eagle* delineated its characteristics: "a bar and [a] sitting room, generally comfortably furnished with mahogany tables and chairs, the walls adorned with pictures and the room well provided with . . . newspapers." The main drink was beer, or rather ale, and there was food, although the eating was incidental to the drinking.

The *Eagle*'s man was careful to emphasize that this sort of bar was English in origin, and indeed there were a number of Englishmen running such places in Brooklyn at the time. But most of the shades were, of course, Irish (an ethnic group the author entirely ignores in his survey of where Brooklyn, which was then largely Irish, liked to drink). If you want to see what a shades looked like in the 1850s, you have but to present yourself at 15 East Seventh Street in Manhattan, where McSorley's still stands today.

These bars did not just serve beer. They also served whiskey. While American whiskey was growing in importance in the 1840s, it still faced strong competition from peach brandy (a uniquely American spirit dating back to the 1600s), which occupied the top of the market; apple brandy (just as old, if a little less prestigious); Dutch-style gin, and New England rum—and those were just the domestic spirits.

The Irish were a whiskey-drinking people, the iconic "pint of plain" having not yet edged it aside as the Emerald Isle's drink of first resort. (That came about in the middle of the century as a result of a national move toward temperance.) In America, they didn't worry too much about securing the stuff from back home: the local rye and bourbon worked just fine, were a hell of a lot cheaper and easier to get, and were much less likely to be adulterated by unscrupulous middlemen. The sheer numbers of newly-minted Irish American drinkers helped swing the dial toward whiskey as America's spirit of choice.

At the time, the standard accompaniment to a shot of whiskey was a little glass of ice water. As the great German American bartender Harry Johnson instructed in his 1882 *New and Improved Bartender's Manual*, "When any party or parties call for any plain or mixed drinks whatever, there must be placed at first before him or them a glass of ice water . . . this rule must not be neglected under any circumstance whatever."

In Ireland, however, if you were going to drink something along with your whiskey, it would be a glass of ale or porter, a pairing dating back to at least the early 1600s. To Americans, this practice seemed odd and dangerous. As late as the 1890s, there are accounts of such an order at a stand-up American bar being greeted with consternation. But by then there were a lot of Irish bars in America, including old, well-established places such as McSorley's (it should be noted that John McSorley, a determinedly temperate man, was firmly opposed to selling anything stronger than ale), McGillin's in Philadelphia (also still operating), Patrick Healy's in Baltimore (later Patrick's of Pratt St., alas now closed), the recently closed and much-lamented Doyle's in South Boston, and James McGarry's in Chicago. These had become city institutions, patronized by all kinds of Americans. The Irish bar was carving out a space for itself in American drinking.

Nobody did more to help it claim this space than a fictional Irishman. Mr. Dooley, who kept a plain little saloon on Archer Road on Chicago's west side, and had an opinion on every event of the day and expressed it in a thick brogue, was the creation of newspaperman Finley Peter Dunne. Dunne based the character on the above James McGarry, whose Dearborn Street saloon drew a lot of reporters, editors, and politicians, none of whom intimidated McGarry in the slightest, as he was sure to let them know in the richest Hibernian English. Dunne introduced Mr. Dooley in 1893 and after a few years of local success, the Dooley columns finally broke through in 1898, becoming something of a national sensation. In the process, however, Mr. Dooley did a great deal to help the Irish saloon become normalized as a part of American culture. What had widely been considered a low doggery, where drunken plug-uglies loitered, waiting for corrupt political bosses to assign them deviltry to do, became—at least among those not beating the drum of Prohibition—a low-to-the ground, no-bullshit workingman's academy, where the drinks were plain and the talk was, too.

Now, Mr. Dooley sold beer and whiskey and never mixed anything more complex than a hot whiskey (alias our old friend, Irish whiskey punch). He had a dim view of cocktails, leaving their concoction "to me frind Schwartzmeister," who kept the saloon down the street and made such productions out of them that all one needed was "a few noodles to look like a biled dinner."

There was more than a grain of truth in this: the massive wave of German immigration that came mid-century, right on the heels of the Irish one, also brought its own drink ways and saloonkeepers. Almost as quickly as Americans came to accept and then clamor for the lager beer the Germans brought with them, the Germans came to appreciate and then master the American art of the bar. By the 1880s, a large proportion of America's most celebrated mixologists were first- or second-generation German immigrants—men such as Henry "Carl" Ramos of gin fizz fame, Harry Johnson, and William "The Only William" Schmidt, the most famous bartender in America—until he was displaced by Mr. Dooley, that is.

But America does things to people. Italians learned to put ravioli in cans, Greeks to grill cheese sandwiches, Afghans to fry chicken, and Hibernians to waltz whiskey or whatever around with bitters—fancy Italian fortified wines—and ice. Beginning in the 1870s, there was an increasing number of Irish bartenders taking up the baton that had fallen from the hands of Murtagh and Alicia Byrne and set out to provide the best of everything in the way of mixed drinks.

The movement first picked up steam in New York at the beginning of the 1880s, when the Hoffman House hotel, which maintained what was generally regarded as the city's premier bar, hired its first Irish bartender. Until that point, it had been staffed by Germans and Americans. Joe McKone (or McKeon) may have been hired for his looks—he was reputed to have been a startlingly handsome young man—but he turned out to be a fine mixologist, inventing, perhaps unsurprisingly, the Adonis cocktail, which is still served today. Before long he was joined by Billy Mullhall, who was "good at making Whiskey Sours" and whose Silver Fizzes were "things of beauty, and joys until the next morning." Before long, Mulhall was head bartender. The bar's most famous helmsman, however, was Charlie Mahoney, who took over in 1897 or thereabouts, having been recruited from John J. Clark's notorious Sixth Avenue dive. That was an unusual move, but Mahoney proved to be both a capable mixologist and a larger-than-life figure in his own right, to match the Hoffman House's famous and sometimes infamous clientele.

In New Orleans, there was Patrick Moran, who contributed cocktail recipes—including an early cousin of the Sazerac—to Lafcadio Hearn's 1885 classic *La Cuisine Creole* and founded the Imperial Cabinet Saloon, later to be taken over by Mr. Ramos. In Rochester, there was Patrick "Patsy" McDonough, "of fame as a mixer of potable liquids," as he was billed. His 1883 book contained some of the earliest fancy cocktails on record, flavored with things such as Bénédictine and Chartreuse. James Maloney, from Chicago, introduced the idea of turning a regular cocktail into a "Bell-Ringer" by serving it in a glass rinsed with apricot brandy. Then there was Tim Daly in Massachusetts and Raymond Sullivan in Baltimore (both of whom also published books), and a double handful of others all across the country.

The most influential hotbed of Irish American mixology, however, was back in New York. In 1897, when the new Astoria hotel was connected to the next-door Waldorf, which had opened in 1893, it included a classic American bar (the Waldorf had been built with only a "café"—basically, a fancy version of a shades, where drinks were served at tables). Michael Killackey was the wine steward and head barman. His crew included John "Curly" O'Connor, from the Waldorf café (he would go on to invent the Bronx cocktail); Johnny Solan (often incorrectly spelled "Solon"); and, in the fullness of time, John Doyle, Phil Kennedy (who kept W. B. Yeats lubricated with Clover Clubs when he stayed at the hotel), Mike Monahan, Ed Murnane, George Gannon, Paddy Hafey, Frank McAloon, and Billy Lahiff (born in Rhode Island to Irish parents). There was also a guy named Terrence—I don't know if that's a first or a last name—and Max Conn, who, for contrast, might have actually been a Kahn (but then again, he might have been a Cohan, like George M.).

I list their names not simply to point and say, "Look at all the Irish," although it's quite the concentration, but by 1910, the bar at "the Hyphen," as the Waldorf-Astoria was known, had taken over from the Hoffman House bar as the leading establishment in America. Its clientele included just about every opinion leader in the country who was still willing to be seen taking a drink in public. In 1914, its influence increased exponentially when Jacob "Jacques" Straub, an Austrian hotelier and wine expert, drew heavily on the bar's private recipes for *Drinks*, the vest-pocket compendium of drink recipes he put together for *The Hotel Monthly*. This little book would serve as the standard reference for a generation of bartenders and become fertile ground for plagiarism for countless other bar books.

But it is instructive to compare the Waldorf's recipes and the ones Charlie Mahoney published in his 1905 *Hoffman House Bartender's Guide*, also a widely popular and oft-reprinted volume, to those of William Schmidt and some of the other German American bartenders who had so defined the mixological arts in the last quarter of the nineteenth century. A drink such as Schmidt's Mayflower (gum syrup, Russian kümmel, brandy, Italian vermouth, crème de cacao, Parfait Amour, and egg yolks), or John Haas's 1904 Modern cocktail (Scotch, sloe gin, lemon juice, absinthe, and two kinds of bitters), or even Ramos's famous gin fizz, with its split lemon and lime juices, cream, and orange flower water, is an exercise in mixological fancy. It aims to surprise and delight.

Drinks at the Hoffman House and, especially, the Waldorf didn't do that. The Irishmen behind the bar brought a bit of Mr. Dooley into their mixology, reeling it in a little lower to the ground. Their drinks tended to be simpler, but also more balanced. They were rarely weird-tasting and never fussy. Take, for instance, the Waldorf's Emerald, an Irish whiskey Manhattan. The boys at the Waldorf bar were among the first to make regular use of Irish whiskey in their cocktails. (James McGarry might have disapproved, but I doubt Murtagh Byrne would.) It might hold few surprises, but it's no less delightful than the aforementioned mixological fancies, and there's practically no fussiness about it.

In 1934, Patrick Gavin Duffy picked up where the Waldorf crew left off. Born in Ballaghaderreen, county Roscommon, Duffy came to New York as a teenager, worked his way up from bellboy to head bartender at the sporty Ashland Hotel on Fourth Avenue, ran a couple of bars of his own, and finally, after going home to Ireland for a decade, settled in Park Slope, Brooklyn. His 1934 *Official Mixer's Manual* was, along with the *Old Mr. Boston Official Bartender's Guide*, one of the foundation stones on which American mixology was rebuilt after Prohibition. In compiling the book, Duffy wrote, he "personally checked every recipe" and "rejected all those not in the best tradition so far as either ingredients, flavor or appeal to the palate are concerned." Where he wasn't sure, he kept the recipe but added a mark to show that he didn't approve.

In thus trimming back some of the more exuberant branches of the cocktail's family tree, Duffy and the other great Irish American bartenders might have made it less ornamental, but they also made it stronger and better adapted to last through the rough winter that, as far as the great American tradition of the bar was concerned, began in 1920 and only ended with the cocktail renaissance of the twenty-first century. The school of mixology that grew back after Prohibition endured the World War II years, the vodka-drenched 1950s, and the mixological Dark Ages of the 1960s, '70s, and '80s (can you say, "martini on the rocks" and "Woo Woo"?), and began to put out fresh shoots in the 1990s was built very largely along the lines laid out by Mahoney, Killackey and his crew, and Duffy. If recent years have seen the tree resume some of that exuberant growth, it's usually coming from branches that were pruned and cared for by Irish hands.

David Wondrich *is one of the world's foremost authorities on the history of the cocktail. A contributing editor at* Esquire *magazine, he is also the author of five books, including* Imbibe!, *the first cocktail book to win a James Beard award.*

Photograph by Doron Guild

"It's not that the Irish are cynical. It's rather that they have a wonderful lack of respect for everything and everybody."

— Brendan Behan

PREFACE

by Sean Muldoon & Jack McGarry

Today we take it as a given that Irish whiskey is an important category of spirit, to be taken as seriously as rum, bourbon, Scotch, gin or tequila. In fact, it's now the fastest-growing spirit category in the world. But that wasn't the situation even as recently as ten years ago in the US. Back then, Irish whiskey was hard to find in any bar. It was obscure, a novelty for Saint Patrick's Day or the occasional (and dependably terrible) Irish Coffee. And definitely not for "proper" cocktails.

The more we learned about Irish whiskey ourselves, the less we understood this state of affairs. Here was a spirit with history and heritage; that boasted real variety in style and flavor; that had terroir. It was exciting, flexible, rewarding. And when it came to cocktails, the potential was vast.

Were we the only ones who could see that? As it turned out, no, we weren't.

Death & Co. is an exceptional cocktail bar in Manhattan. It had been operating for about six years before we opened the Dead Rabbit, and in that time had acquired a serious reputation for the quality of its cocktails. When we first visited, the bar had recently appointed a new head bartender named Jillian Vose. Jillian had just completed a new menu of original drinks. To our astonishment, it contained a section called Paddy Drinks: extraordinarily well-considered and well-executed cocktails based around bottlings like Clontarf, Redbreast 12, and Connemara peated. It was a revelation. We became friends with Jillian and spent a lot of time talking about whiskey.

But that name. Paddy Drinks.

It bothered us. Sure, it was just common American bartender shorthand for a cocktail that happened to feature Irish whiskey. There was no intention to malign Irish people,

PADDY DRINKS

Conamara Cocktail

Connemara Peated Irish Whiskey,
Green Chartreuse, Cocchi
Torino Vermouth, Campari,
Cinnamon Syrup {$16}

Enemies of Promise

Clontarf 1814 Irish Whiskey,
Fresh Lemon Juice, Acaçia Honey
Syrup, Fresh Curry Leaves,
Quince Preserves {$14}

Sunshine Lady

Kilbeggan Irish Whiskey, Hibiscus
Honey Syrup, Wray & Nephew Over
Proof Rhum, Aperol, Peychaud's
Bitters, Egg Yolk {$14}

San Patricia's Battalion

Redbreast 12 Year Irish Whiskey,
Dolin Blanc Vermouth,
Del Maguey Chichicapa Mezcal,
St. Germain {$15}

> **"God invented Whiskey to keep the Irish
> from ruling the world."**
> •••
> **WILLIAM FAULKNER**

Image by Kate and Tim Tomkinson

like us, who bristle at all things paddywhackery, plastic shamrocks, leprechauns, and the like, to be sure, to be sure. The implicit dismissiveness in the term "Paddy" was reflective of an attitude that saw no real quality or refinement within the drinks—because Irish whiskey was more or less, give or take, all in all, generally speaking, taking everything into consideration, to a large degree . . . well, the same. Which is to say, nothing special.

But that was never was true, never will be. So we decided to get even, by reclaiming Paddy Drinks as a category that deserves—no, demands—respect on its own merits. The whiskey we know is gloriously subtle and distinctive, offering a vast panorama of flavors and aromas. And in the hands of a skilled bartender, Irish whiskey is capable of producing truly sublime mixed drinks. (These pages are, we believe, proof of that.)

The Christmas Eve after we opened, Jillian visited the bar as a guest and brought along her mother. When we were introduced, we realized that Jillian's mother was Irish. Not Irish American, but Irish Irish. So Jillian knew the country and knew where we were from, and over the years had spent a lot of time in Ireland visiting her family. It was another thing we had in common. But there was more: whiskey. Here was someone way ahead of the curve and on our wavelength, making our national spirit relevant and interesting and utterly contemporary.

Not long afterward, fate intervened and an opening arose unexpectedly for a head bartender at the Dead Rabbit. When we sat down to consider a replacement, we had only one name on our list. She took a little persuading—which is a story for another day—but eventually, Jillian said yes. Then we raised our glasses to yesterday, today, and tomorrow, and as one, said the only thing that needed to be said:

Slainte!

INTRODUCTION

by Jillian Vose

At one time, people would have had you believe that whiskey is whiskey is whiskey. Those people were wrong, wrong, wrong. Now, it's certainly the case that this dismissive attitude prevailed when we first started to look at Irish whiskey in cocktails. But the more we looked, the more we realized that there's a world of difference to be discovered and enjoyed here—and the drinks we've created for this book are the proof.

Here at the Dead Rabbit, Irish whiskey is a fundamental part of what we're all about. We believe in it; we're committed to it. Always will be. We're still teaching ourselves and we're also still learning—because the category is truly endless. You'll never know it all. But finding out is half the fun, right?

So how do you make great drinks with Irish whiskey? What makes the stuff different and special? How is it made and blended? How does maturation affect flavor? Why one style rather than another?

These are just some of the key questions this book will answer. If you're a bartender, you'll learn how to use all the categories, exploring their distinctive characteristics to the fullest in order to create your own outstanding original cocktails. What's more, your guests stand to benefit, too, as you help them discover new drinks they'll really love.

And if you're an amateur mixologist, you'll find plenty to interest and engage you here. In addition to step-by-step guides, methods, and tips, we've got ninety drinks for you, arranged into four categories: Single Grain, Single Malt, Single Pot Still, and Blended. These are recipes we've featured at the Dead Rabbit over the years, and together they help demonstrate the extraordinary versatility of Irish whiskey.

In each category, we'll also discuss how that style is produced and aged and what makes it distinctive. We'll also offer some tasting notes and even list some key bottlings for you to seek out. A flavor wheel provides a visual explanation of how to identify and analyze flavors, and how we use these to create our modern Irish whiskey cocktails. Which means you can, too.

Everybody ready? OK, then—let's go . . .

THE IRISH PUB
AS WOODEN HORSE

by Sean Muldoon and Jack McGarry

Irish pubs have shaped New York's drinking culture ever since . . . well, ever since the Irish have been coming here in number—which is to say, first in the 1820s and then the 1840s, during the Famine (or "Great Hunger"). They've been a constant presence in a constantly shifting landscape. We knew we were part of a great tradition. But in itself, that wouldn't be enough to succeed. So when we came to New York, it was with a plan. A plan as old as antiquity. It was a Trojan horse. We intended to smuggle in the world's best cocktail bar within the cozy surroundings of a traditional old Irish pub. And it worked. The Dead Rabbit won the highest accolades, the admiration and respect of our peers, but, more importantly, it earned the enthusiastic appreciation of visitors from all over the world.

In 2017, the British newspaper the *Guardian* visited the bar and declared, "The Dead Rabbit takes a time-honored tradition of hospitality, a sense of history, and young dynamic staff, and turns them into a modern Irish Bar that is accessible, irresistible, even fiercely romantic."

We were flattered, but also pleased that our intentions had been so transparently realized. Because our ambitions have now changed. We're on a mission again, this time to restore the reputation of the authentic Irish pub, to rescue it from its ersatz "Plastic Paddy" iterations. We want to open an Irish pub in several major cities in the US, and have each one be known as the best Irish pub in that city. By best, we mean with the best-trained and informed staff, best décor, best product offering, best hospitality, period. Irish whiskey will be absolutely central to the execution of that plan, which we think of as bringing the Irish pub forward into the twenty-first century.

And so, you may ask, will that plan use another Trojan horse? Ah now, that would be telling.

THE DEAD RABBIT AND IRISH WHISKEY:

HOW AN EDUCATION BECAME AN OBSESSION

by Sean Muldoon and Jack McGarry

We'll start with a confession—an embarrassing one, as confessions tend to be. When we were planning the Dead Rabbit, one of the features we were most insistent upon was a great collection of Irish whiskey bottles that would line the back bar. As an Irish bar out to make its mark, this would be our calling card.

But—and here's the confession—we didn't actually know that much about what was in those bottles. Sure, we knew the famous whiskey names and labels, but frankly, not much more. Not about its extraordinary variety, its history, how it's made, aged, blended. None of that.

Then a couple of things happened. When we were still researching the Dead Rabbit, we visited dozens and dozens of places in New York, everything from dive bars to high-end cocktail palaces. And nowhere seemed to have any Irish whiskey, other than perhaps the odd bottle gathering dust. When we asked why, we were told there was no demand for the stuff except for the occasional Saint Patrick's Day shot or the infamous pickleback (a measure of Jameson followed by a sip of chilled pickle juice).

What's more, it was the same story everywhere.

In fact, in one famous cocktail bar, we were told the manager wouldn't even let Irish whiskey sully his shelves. That's how little he respected it. In that case, we asked, how do you make an Irish Coffee—a classic cocktail? With bourbon, came the brazen reply. It was an outrage, a travesty, an affront, a scandal. A sign.

One day, not long after the Dead Rabbit opened, a server took an order for eight Irish Coffees, a drink we'd always intended to feature. But we weren't set up to handle multiple servings at the same time. The result was a mess. We swore we'd never get caught out like that again. This kick-started our search for a system to produce the drink perfectly —and consistently. (More about that later.)

The Dead Rabbit was busy from the start. Word had gotten around about this amazing young Irish bartender, and people flocked in just to see Jack work his cocktail magic. Meanwhile, most of the media and trade interviews focused on Sean. The journalists were annoyingly well-informed and knowledgeable. Sean was often asked about that impressive Irish whiskey collection, about pot still whiskey versus single malt, about distillation and rectification, about how much malt is in the Bushmills Black Bush blend, if Irish whiskey is always triple-distilled. They assumed he was an expert. He wasn't. Far from it. For a time, he bluffed, but that couldn't last. It was clear that we needed an education—and fast. While Sean focused on publicizing and running this exciting new bar, Jack went back to Ireland and did a tour of the distilleries operating at the time: Cooley, Kilbeggan, Bushmills, and Midleton. He met the master distillers and blenders, and discovered single grains, single malts, single pot stills, and blends. He learned history and methods, and he took lots and lots of notes.

On his return, he and Sean pooled this knowledge and structured it into a training program for staff. In this way, servers could help guests make informed choices about drinks and cocktails.

And we kept going.

Our first menu concentrated on historic and overlooked drinks categories. For our second, we shifted the focus to our own original drinks. Many of them featured Irish whiskey. We were learning and putting that learning into practice.

We introduced "flights"—samples of different whiskeys with tasting notes, so that guests could start to discern the differences among styles.

And we invested. We opened our Irish Whiskey Academy on the bar's third floor, a sort of training school where guests and trade alike could discover what they'd been missing.

In time we replaced the old training module with our Irish Whiskey Genius course, and we made it compulsory for all bar and floor staff. There are four components: a series of ten online modules, a prescribed reading list, a tasting test, and a final written exam. Pass it, and you get an all-expenses paid trip to Ireland, complete with distillery and pub tours. Not a bad incentive, right?

"WE SHOULD WRITE THIS DOWN."

In 2018, we made a serious decision. We went home. And we hit the road. We embarked on two all-Ireland trips, visiting every available distillery (including some that were still in the planning stage) and over 160 of the country's finest traditional hostelries. The result was a book, *From Barley to Blarney*, that we describe as a love letter to our twin obsessions: Irish whiskey and Irish pubs.

It came about, as many of the best ideas do, over a pint of Guinness in a pub. In fact, over many pints and in many pubs. For years Sean had been visiting the country's old bars, often in the company of Midleton's master cooper, Ger Buckley. From time to time on these "research trips," he'd bump into an old friend, Tim Herlihy, the US brand ambassador for Tullamore D.E.W., and they'd all talk whiskey and pubs. "We should put all this together some time and write it all down," someone would say, then order another round. But eventually we did. It was quite a slog. It's also quite a read.

A WHISKEY OF OUR OWN

When people see a bottle of Dead Rabbit Irish Whiskey, they sometimes ask if we've just lent our name to it. Absolutely not. Given our preoccupation (OK, obsession) with the spirit, that's the last thing we'd do. Our whiskey is, as the label says, dreamed, distilled, and matured in Dublin—in a distillery in the Liberties, the dynamic quarter that was the historic center of Ireland's once mighty whiskey-making industry. And we were part of its creation from the very start and every step of the way. That's why you see our signatures on every bottle.

It's a blend of malt and grain whiskeys aged for at least five years in ex-bourbon barrels and then finished in small virgin oak casks. The taste is complex, malty, and spicy—a true Irish whiskey heart with strong overtones of bourbon and vanilla.

You can enjoy Dead Rabbit Irish Whiskey neat, on the rocks, or in a cocktail. And you'll find it featured in several recipes throughout the book—strictly on its own merits, too.

LEARNING MORE AND SPREADING THE WORD

In 2019, we launched the New York Irish Whiskey Festival. It was a two-day sold-out event. Word had clearly been getting around.

Meanwhile, we're constantly refining our systems, deepening our knowledge. And what about that whiskey collection? It's now the largest in the US and one of the biggest in the world. We soon realized it was more random than considered; it lacked structure and shape, and there were big gaps. So we set about rebuilding it, making it coherent. Making it make sense. Because now we knew better, and we wanted to do better. We still do. The water of life deserves it.

Photograph by Elaine Hill

A LITTLE HISTORY

Distilling in Ireland began in the mists of antiquity: some sources suggest as far back as the sixth century. What we do know is that for many centuries its techniques and practice were the preserve of religious orders. From the earliest days, the spirit produced was known as *uisce beatha* (pronounced ISH-ka BA-ha), which means "water of life" in Irish. As Ireland became more anglicized, that pronunciation evolved into "whiskey."

For a long time—a really long time, in fact—the word "whiskey" meant one thing only: pot still. It is our unique and quintessential style and, some would say, the jewel among Irish whiskeys. It is pot still that once dominated the world of whiskey, and indeed even other spirits. And it is pot still that was almost lost forever.

In 1887, English journalist Alfred Barnard published his opus *The Whisky Distilleries of the United Kingdom*. In the Irish section, Barnard lists twenty-eight distilleries. Of these, twenty-six were solely occupied with making pot still whiskey, such was the global demand. Yet within a century, pot still, in all its full-bodied, velvety, creamy, gingery-spicy loveliness, was gone. Gone into history, into myth. Well, almost. Because whiskey time is a bit like geological time: on another scale altogether. Or, to borrow another analogy, the pot still story resembles those rare plants that seem to have vanished from the earth, only to waken from their long sleep and erupt suddenly into extravagant bloom once again. Irish pot still is back. Not, of course, on the same scale as in its world-bestriding Victorian heyday, but back nonetheless, made with care and love by distillers dedicated to restoring the full glories of the true and blissful spirit.

IRISH WHISKEY
A LITTLE HISTORY

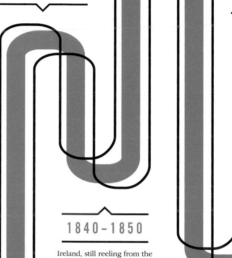

1100s

By this time, Irish monks had discovered alembics, other distillation equipment, and, crucially, knowledge of their use for creating botanical extracts and perfumes, as well as tinctures and elixirs, primarily for me-dicinal purposes. Gradually, however, the monks began to use local cereal crops in place of flowers and fruits.

1405

The Annals of the Four Masters—a series of chronicles of medieval Irish his-tory—records the first explicit mention of whiskey in the poignant account of the sad demise of one Richard Magrenell through "a surfeit of aquae vi-tae [uisce beatha]" at Christmas.

1608

King James I awards the first distilling license to a local landowner in the place that will later be the home of the Bushmills distillery in county Antrim. Whether or not that landowner distilled anything in 1608 is another matter, though there was certainly a long history of (mostly illicit) distilling there on the beautiful Causeway Coast.

1770s

The British impose taxes on malted barley. In response, the Irish begin distilling using a mixture of malted and unmalted barley—and in the process, invent pot still whiskey.

1830

Former Inspector General of excise turned distiller Aeneas Coffey invents a still that enables continuous distillation—a radical shift from the slow, traditional approach. However, major Irish whiskey-makers decline to adopt it, disparaging its product as "silent spirit" and even unworthy of the name whiskey. Scottish distillers, however, are more receptive to Coffey's invention. At this time, Irish whiskey is the world's spirit of choice—making it a highly important as well as lucrative export.

1840–1850

Ireland, still reeling from the Famine, sees its whiskey industry decline steeply. The repeal of the Corn Laws in 1846 triggers an influx of cheap American corn, from which the Coffey still produces a neutral spirit that is mixed with traditional pot still, giving rise to blended whiskey. This is instantly popular in Britain, further eroding a prime market for Irish pot still.

1900s

Scottish distilleries see continued growth in blended whisky, and its Distillers Company Limited conglomerate opens its own distillery in Dublin.

1909

In defining "whiskey," a Royal Commission approves Scottish-style Coffey distillation, pitting the increasingly popular and lighter grain whiskey against the heavier traditional pot still.

1916–1930

This period sees three major events, each one of which has a serious impact on the Irish whiskey industry. Scottish Coffey stills create a surplus and prices collapse. At home, Ireland's bitter Civil War erupts and distilling ceases as all barley is required for the war effort. And in the US, the Volstead Act is passed, enforcing Prohibition—and, at a stroke, eliminating a huge market for Irish whiskey.

1988

Irish Distillers is acquired by Pernod Ricard, which helps consolidate Jameson as the world's largest-selling Irish whiskey. Midleton also begins to revive old brands, along with Tullamore D.E.W., Redbreast, and the famous Spot series.

1975

IDL opens a new state-of-the-art distillery in Midleton in Cork. The Jameson, Powers, and old Midleton distilleries close.

2010

Despite growing demand, there are still only four distilleries producing Irish whiskey: Cooley, Kilbeggan, New Midleton, and Old Bushmills.

1950s–60s

By 1953, there are only six distilleries left on the island, largely serving only domestic demand: Jameson and Powers in Dublin, Cork Distilleries Company (CDC) in Cork, Tullamore distillery in Offaly, and the Bushmills and Coleraine distilleries in Northern Ireland. Meanwhile, Scotch flourishes in the US, completely eclipsing Irish whiskey.

2020

There are over thirty operational distilleries, with projections totaling around fifty within the next five to ten years.

1999–2000

Demand returns for all traditional styles of Irish whiskey—pot still, single malt, blended, and single grain.

1933

The end of Prohibition releases pent-up demand, which the now-devastated Irish industry is unable to meet. But the Scottish distillers can. Also, Ireland enters into a ruinous trade war with Britain, culminating in its exclusion to 25 percent of world markets.

1966

There are now only four distilleries left. Then, in what is effectively a last roll of the dice for the Irish industry, Jameson, Powers, and Cork merge to form Irish Distillers Limited (IDL). Bushmills holds out until 1973, then joins.

1987

John Teeling converts a semi-derelict former industrial alcohol plant outside Dundalk into Cooley Distillery. It's Ireland's first new purpose-built whiskey distillery in around a century. Among other things—including reviving some old Kilbeggan brands—this presents a challenge to the near monopoly enjoyed by IDL.

2015

Teeling Distillery opens in Dublin—in The Liberties, in fact, the former engine room of the great Irish distilling industry. It is the first new Irish whiskey distillery to open in over 125 years.

"IRISH WHISKEY IS NOW THE FASTEST-GROWING SPIRIT IN THE WORLD"

"WHISKEY IS IRISH. IT REALLY CANNOT BE MADE TO THE SAME QUALITY ANYWHERE ELSE IN THE WORLD. IT IS THE IRISH CLIMATE. IRISH WATER IS GOOD, AS IS THE BARLEY, BUT IT IS THE CLIMATE THAT GIVES IRISH WHISKEY THE UNIQUE MELLOW FLAVOR ... THE OAK BARRELS BREATHE IN THE GENTLE CLIMATE. TOO HOT, LIKE THE US IN SUMMER, AND THE OAK EXPANDS, ALLOWING QUICKER AND HARSHER MATURATION. TOO COLD, LIKE CANADA AND SCOTLAND, AND THE OAK CLOSES UP, REDUCING MATURATION. A MOIST CLIMATE BRUSHED BY TEMPERATE WINDS FROM THE GULF STREAM COMING IN FROM THE ATLANTIC IS PERFECT."

— JOHN TEELING, 2010 COOLEY DISTILLERY ANNUAL REPORT

WHAT MAKES IT SPECIAL?

Now, you may think that Mr. Teeling is somewhat biased, but if anyone is entitled to make such a claim, it's him. As the maverick founder of both the Cooley and Great Northern Distilleries, he played a major role in the rescue of Irish whiskey in the 1980s—and in its subsequent revival. He is also right. Irish whiskey is special. We recognize that now, though perhaps we did not always. That's part of the story of how after the glory days in the nineteenth century, when Irish pot still was the world's spirit of choice, we almost lost the industry completely. As you read in the preceding timeline, it was a near miss of gigantic proportions; indeed, there were several near misses. And so, duly chastened, we resolved as a nation to set the industry on an even keel, once and for all. Well, as best we could.

A MATTER OF PRIDE (OH, AND IT'S THE LAW)

It's fair to say that in Ireland we've always enjoyed our whiskey, but we haven't always taken the industry that produced it very seriously. But it truly is a matter of great national pride—one of our gifts to the world, along with Guinness and an extravagant, carefree way with English (the language of the old oppressor).

Having nearly lost the whole shebang, today we're witnessing this great industry rise once again. That current upward trajectory is where we'd like to keep it.

One way we've done that is the creation of the Irish Whiskey Association (IWA), a body that represents the industry and exists to promote and protect Irish whiskey at home and overseas. It was formed to help streamline the processes that allow new distilleries to open, and to set up mentorship programs between the traditional operators and the start-ups. Its efforts include "registration of Irish whiskey as a geographical indication, appellation of origin, collective trademark or certification trademark."

And there's more. Much more. Take this lot from the October 2014 Irish Whiskey Technical File, produced by the IWA in conjunction with the Irish government's Department of Agriculture, Food and the Marine:

> *"Irish Whiskey/Uisce Beatha Eireannach/Irish Whisky" cannot be labelled, packaged, sold, advertised or promoted in a way that includes any reference to a period of maturation or age of the whiskey unless it is to the period of maturation or age of the youngest whiskey in the drink expressed in years and consisting of one number (which may be expressed either as a numeral or as a word), and provided that the whiskey was aged under appropriate control and verification.*
>
> *The term 'Single' can only be applied to the varieties of "Pot Still Irish Whiskey/Irish Pot Still Whiskey", "Malt Irish Whiskey/Irish Malt Whiskey" and "Grain Irish Whiskey/Irish Grain Whiskey", provided all of the whiskey in the product is distilled totally on the site of a single distillery and comes from one of these three varieties.*
>
> *All Irish whiskeys must bear the sales denomination "Irish Whiskey" or "Uisce Beatha Eireannach" or "Irish Whisky", unless they qualify as "Pot Still Irish Whiskey/Irish Pot Still Whiskey" or "Malt Irish Whisky/Irish Malt Whiskey" or "Grain Irish Whiskey/Irish Grain Whiskey" or "Blended Irish Whiskey/", in which event they must bear the relevant sales denomination.*

That's the law, you know. And that's before we even get to the strictures on labeling, which run on for several hundred lines as well.

So, as you can see, we've gotten serious about the serious stuff. Which is good for us, and even better for you, because it means each bottle labeled "Irish whiskey" conforms to strict regulations about style, production, aging, and origin. All of which, in due course, makes its way into the glass in your hand and the liquid amber within.

HOW IT'S MADE

We live in a world of many whiskeys, whiskies, and, indeed, whiskys. Produced everywhere from Ireland and Scotland to North America, continental Europe and Scandinavia, South Africa, India, Australia, New Zealand, and Japan (and pretty much everywhere in between), they vary hugely in style, flavor, balance, finish, color, and so on. But—and here's the important thing—they are all made in more or less the same way. Which is to say, the way whiskey has always been made, using grain, yeast, water, and, of course, the fourth essential ingredient: time.

On the face of it, the process is straightforward: a cereal grain is mashed into a beer. That beer is distilled and then aged. And, well, that's about it. Except of course, it isn't. That simplistic description masks a vastly more complex truth. Considerable skill and experience are required to make the stuff, for within each of those basic steps lie myriad variations and possibilities. What strain of yeast to use, what grain (and should it be malted or unmalted), where is the water from, how long should fermentation last, in what type of wooden cask will the whiskey be left to age?

And so whiskey-making becomes every bit as much art as science.

But let's look at the process in a little more detail, remembering that at every stage the distiller has decisions and choices to make, all of which can potentially have a significant effect on the flavor of the whiskey. It can be broken down into four main stages (which themselves have numerous parts): brewing, fermentation, distillation, and maturation.

We start with the grain: barley—or, more accurately, malted barley. This is a crucial ingredient in Irish whiskey. Now, malting is interesting for two very important reasons. First, for what it achieves in the whiskey-making process. And second, for its crucial role in the history of Irish whiskey and the creation of its most iconic style, pot still (see Timeline, page 30). For now, though, let's look at its part in production.

Malting is, in effect, a trick played on the grain. A trick that says, "Rise and shine—summer has arrived." By steeping the barley in water, the distiller fools the seed into germinating, marked by the sprouting of short green tendrils. This means the seed's stored-up starches are being converted into sugars, which, when brought into contact with yeast, will produce alcohol. Drying the barley—a process called kilning—stops germination at just the right moment and allows the distiller to access the sugar.

First, though, the sprouting grain is milled to a coarse, flourlike substance called grist. It is placed in a vessel called a mash tun and hot water is added, triggering the all-important conversion of starch into sugar. The resulting sugary liquid is known as wort. It is drained through the perforated base of the mash tun, and the process is repeated for maximum extraction of the sugar. The now spent grains, or draff, are often sold as animal feed.

Next, the wort is pumped into the fermenters (also called washbacks) and yeast is added. The yeast effectively gobbles up the available sugar in the barley and, in doing so, creates alcohol (primarily ethanol), along with carbon dioxide and hundreds of other compounds called congeners that are critical in contributing aroma, flavor, and texture to the whiskey. In fact, most of the floral, fruity, herbal, and/or spicy flavors that you might detect in Irish whiskey are introduced at this stage—fermentation—by the yeast. At this juncture, things get very lively in the still. When the cloudy mixture stops frothing, fermentation is complete, leaving a yeasty-smelling unhopped beer that is around 9 percent alcohol by volume (ABV).

The purpose of distillation itself is to concentrate the alcohol content of the wash. In Ireland, all whiskey is at least double-distilled, and much of it is triple-distilled.

All this takes place either in a traditional copper pot still or a continuous column still. Next, the wort is boiled. The alcohol vaporizes at a lower temperature than water and these so-called "low wines" are collected for further distillation. The process is repeated two or three times, removing water and impurities each time, the alcoholic vapor being condensed and recirculated.

At last, the new-make spirit is ready for the final stage of production: maturation. It can be argued with some justification that this is the most important step in the making of whiskey, and for one very good reason: this is where much of the flavor of the finished whiskey comes from.

So, does all the spirit produced during distillation go into the barrel? Definitely not. The first part of the spirit produced in the still contains unpleasant-tasting elements that would contaminate the maturing whiskey. Likewise, the thinner, weaker spirit created at the end of distillation is not really drinkable. So, the part that is needed for casking is the middle "cut," also known as the heart. This is what ultimately finds its way from the still into the barrel.

Ah, the barrel. Now things get even more interesting. Here slow chemical reactions take place that gradually change the flavors in the whiskey. Since the wooden staves of the barrels are porous, the new-make spirit soaks into them, drawing out color, tannins, caramelized wood sugars, and flavor compounds. Oxygen from the outside air will also enter the barrel as it "breathes" and slowly oxidizes the spirit, rounding out and developing its flavors.

THE ROLE OF WOOD

Traditionally, the barrels or casks used for maturing Irish whiskey are made of oak and have previously held bourbon or sherry. These are the two most common former inhabitants of the casks before whiskey moves in. These days, however, we are increasingly seeing ex-rum, Madeira, Cognac, and port pipes quite frequently used—as you will discover in this book.

The choice of cask is crucial, because the spirit or wine that was previously in the barrel can greatly influence the color and taste of the maturing whiskey. This makes cask selection a keen area for experimentation and innovation, with today's distillers trying everything from ex-aquavit and Japanese sake barrels to Calvados. Another way of maximizing that influence is through charring the inside of the barrel. This "opens up" the wood, giving the alcohol access to soluble—and desirable—flavor compounds within. Ex-bourbon casks are made from American oak, which imparts aromas reminiscent of vanilla and spice. Former sherry casks are made from European oak, which lends notes of dried fruit, cloves, and walnut. By cask-finishing the whiskey—essentially a short second period of aging—in another type of wood, such as Madeira or port, the distiller can also add another layer to the character of the finished whiskey.

BLENDING

So, then, is this now mature whiskey ready for bottling? Yes. No. Maybe. In fact, all things considered, probably no. That's because we now enter one of the most mysterious and arcane parts of the whiskey-making process: blending.

It's been said that if distilling is the science, blending is the art. Two seemingly identical casks filled with the same liquid can produce very different results, partly because the nature of the wood varies from one barrel to another, and partly because, well, there are just so many variables at play. The source of the barrel, how many times it was used before, even the tree it was cut from, these factors will all contribute toward making each cask—and therefore the whiskey maturing inside it—unique.

OTHER FACTORS: WAREHOUSING AND WEATHER

Maturing whiskey is surprisingly sensitive to temperature and will actually age faster in a warmer climate than a cold one. This is the case even where microclimates are involved, as in a small country like Ireland. Indeed, master distiller Barry Crockett noticed that when he worked at the Midleton distillery in county Cork in the (fractionally warmer) southern part of Ireland, the whiskey matured quicker than in the Bushmills distillery in the (fractionally colder) north. Furthermore, the atmospheric conditions can also affect flavor: a whiskey maturing in a warehouse near the coast will tend to develop a slightly salty edge. This is a result of the porous nature of the barrels in which the spirit was aged.

If you are trying to make a whiskey to a very specific profile—such as, for example, Bushmills Black Bush or Tullamore D.E.W.—controlling those variables and producing a consistent spirit really is where the art and science converge in the work of the master distiller and blender. It's a problem with only one solution: an extraordinary palate combined with years and years of experience.

BOTTLING

When the mature whiskey is ready to be bottled, there are still a couple of decisions to be made. One is chill filtering. This is a slightly controversial area. Some whiskey aficionados abhor it; other experts confidently maintain it has no discernible effect on flavor whatsoever. But, what is it? When whiskey is finally ready to be decanted from the barrel into the bottle, it is often slightly cloudy. The cloudiness is caused by organic compounds (congener oils). If left on a shelf, these will, in time, settle into a kind of sediment at the bottom of the bottle. Some brands consider this unsightly and undesirable. So before they bottle the whiskey, the distillers chill it and filter it to remove these organic compounds. This will prevent the whiskey from going cloudy, but can also affect mouthfeel. Or not.

It's become enough of an issue in whiskey-world that some brands now make a point of adding "non-chill-filtered" to their labels. (If there's no such reference, it's fair to assume that the whiskey has been chill-filtered.) As far as we're concerned, the more information on a label, the better.

If a standard color is required—which would be the case, say, for a major branded whiskey —spirit caramel may be added at the bottling stage. Again, although widespread, this practice has its detractors. The last consideration is strength, or alcohol by volume (ABV). Legally, Irish whiskey must be a minimum of 40% ABV, and so the mature whiskey will be diluted down to this point, which is known as "cask strength."

A WORD ABOUT AGE STATEMENTS

The age statement on a bottle of Irish whiskey indicates the youngest whiskey that is included in the blend. A bottle of Redbreast 12 contains whiskeys up to fourteen years old, but the label tells us that the youngest whiskey in the blend is twelve years old. With single malt and single pot still whiskeys, the age statement again refers to the youngest whiskey in the bottle, which in this case is also the oldest whiskey in the bottle, as there's only one.

"AND NOW, THE NAS"

You've just read that the age statement highlights the youngest whiskey in a blend. When that whiskey is being blended with, say, a twenty-year-old whiskey, a potential problem arises. A marketing problem. Can a brand command a premium price for a mostly-twenty-year-old whiskey whose label suggests it's actually four years old?

One solution is NAS: the non-age statement. This is used in whiskeys with a specific age statement, such as Jameson Black Barrel and the Jameson Caskmates expressions. In these cases, the whiskeys have been produced to highlight a certain characteristic, such as the charring of the cask or type of cask wood used. The NAS allows the distiller to focus on what really, truly matters about what's inside the bottle: It's not the age of the whiskey. It's the taste.

STYLES OF IRISH WHISKEY

In Ireland, we distill three very distinct styles of whiskey: pot still, malt, and grain. A fourth style, blended, features a combination of two or more of the other three. The production of each of the three styles is different, and for a distillery to make all three would entail a vast investment of money, time, equipment, and expertise. Therefore, the big distilleries often sell distillate to one another so that they don't have to make each component themselves. For example, Midleton produces both pot still whiskey and grain whiskey, and will sell unaged grain distillate to Bushmills for use in its blends. Bushmills produces malt whiskey but no grain or pot still whiskey, and will supply Midleton with malt distillate to use in its blends. And so on. It's also the case that more brands are opening up their own distilleries and producing their own new-make spirit. As with all things whiskey, it comes down to a question of time.

SINGLE GRAIN WHISKEY

Unlike pot still and malts, grain whiskey is distilled using a column still. This produces a spirit that is lighter and cleaner in body, almost delicate; sweeter in taste, and more floral on the nose. It is most often distilled from a base of corn (maize), with some malted barley added, although this isn't a requirement. Other grains such as wheat or oats may also be used. A single grain Irish whiskey is only the grain component distilled and matured by itself. Midleton and Cooley currently account for most of the grain whiskey made in Ireland.

KEY BOTTLINGS

Kilbeggan single grain, Teeling single grain, The Busker, Clonakilty Bordeaux cask (Connacht Distillery), Egan's vintage grain, Glendalough Double Barrel, Ballyhoo

SINGLE MALT WHISKEY

Malt whiskey must be produced from 100 percent malted barley. Like pot still, it is double- or triple-distilled in copper pot stills. To qualify as single malt, the whiskey must be made solely at one distillery. Currently, the Bushmills and Cooley distilleries produce the greatest volumes of single malt in Ireland. They also provide malt whiskey to other distilleries for use in blends. Irish single malts are typically soft and creamy in texture and "bready" or "biscuity" in their flavor profile.

KEY BOTTLINGS

Bushmills single malt expressions, Knappogue Castle single malt expressions, Connemara 12 single malt, Teeling single malt, West Cork expressions, Tyrconnell expressions, The Sexton, Egan's expressions

SINGLE POT STILL WHISKEY

This style, unique to Ireland, is made from a mash of both malted and unmalted barley, which gives pot still its characteristic full, spicy, rounded flavor and creamy texture. In addition to the barley, the mash may contain up to 5 percent of other cereal grains, such as rye or oats. The mash is fermented and then double- or triple-distilled in copper pot stills.

KEY BOTTLINGS

Redbreast expressions; Powers John's Lane and Powers Three Swallow; Midleton Barry Crockett Legacy; the Spot series (Green Spot, Yellow Spot, and Red Spot), Blue Spot, Drumshanbo, Teeling, The Busker

BLENDED WHISKEY

A blended Irish whiskey is not, by definition, inferior to a single grain, single malt, or pot still whiskey. The success of the blend comes down to the quality of the constituent whiskeys and the skill of the blender. Blends are often light and accessible when grain whiskey is included in the mix, while the addition of pot still or malt whiskey will lend body and complexity. Blended whiskeys—such as Jameson Original—can be a wonderful gateway into the world of Irish whiskey, when a single pot still or single malt whiskey might be too rich or intense.

KEY BOTTLINGS

Pot still and grain: Jameson expressions, Powers Gold Label, Clontarf, Kilbeggan

Malt and grain: Bushmills Black Bush, Teeling Small Batch, Writers' Tears Copper Pot, Dead Rabbit, Dubliner bourbon cask, Slane, Roe & Co, Pearse Lyons 'The Original', Clonakilty port cask, Hinch Small Batch

Pot still and malt: The Irishman Founder's Reserve; Writers' Tears

Pot still, malt, and grain: Tullamore D.E.W. blends, Paddy, The Busker 'Triple Cask Triple Smooth', Pearse Lyons 5-year-old and 7-year-old, Dead Rabbit, The Dubliner expressions, Clonakilty expressions, Connacht expressions, Hinch expressions, Slane, Kilbegggan, Roe & Co., Teeling Blackpitts

UNDERSTANDING THE EXPRESSIONS OF IRISH WHISKEY

In order to pair flavors with different whiskeys, you first you have to understand each whiskey by picking out its unique characteristics. We do that by looking at the liquid's aromas and taste qualities. These graphs will help guide you through the different styles of Irish whiskey by identifying essential characteristics, their connections, and the effect of combining them.

Graphics by Marcus Lynam

No.	Whiskey
01.	Bushmills 10 yo single malt
02.	Bushmills 16 yo single malt
03.	Bushmills Black Bush
04.	Bushmills Red Bush
05.	Clonakilty Bordeaux cask
06.	Clonakilty double oak
07.	Clonakilty port cask
08.	Egan's single grain
09.	Glendolaugh pot still
10	Green Spot pot still
11.	Jameson IPA cask
12.	Jameson stout cask
13.	Kilbeggan rye
14.	Kilbeggan single grain
15.	Knappogue 12 yo single malt
16.	Knappogue 14 yo single malt
17.	Method & Madness single grain
18.	Method & Madness pot still
19.	Method & Madness single malt
20.	Paddy Irish whiskey
21.	Powers John's Lane
22.	Powers Three Swallow
23.	Redbreast 12 yo pot still
24.	Redbreast Lustau
25.	Slane Irish whiskey
26.	Teeling pot still (2nd batch)
27.	Teeling single grain
28.	Teeling Small Batch
29.	Tullamore D.E.W. Caribbean cask
30.	Tullamore D.E.W. cider cask
31.	Tullamore D.E.W. Original
32.	Tyrconnell 10 yo Madeira cask
33.	Tyrconnell 10 yo sherry cask
34.	Tyrconnell 10 yo port cask
35.	Tyrconnell ex-bourbon cask
36.	West Cork bog oak
37.	West Cork ex-bourbon cask
38.	West Cork peated
39.	Writers' Tears pot still
40.	Yellow Spot pot still

THE X/Y CHART

Here, we've very helpfully tabulated the key bottlings mentioned above, showing where each broadly sits, for example Light, Complex, Rich, or Delicate. Think of it as a handy way to home in on the right whiskey for a drink you're trying to create. You're welcome.

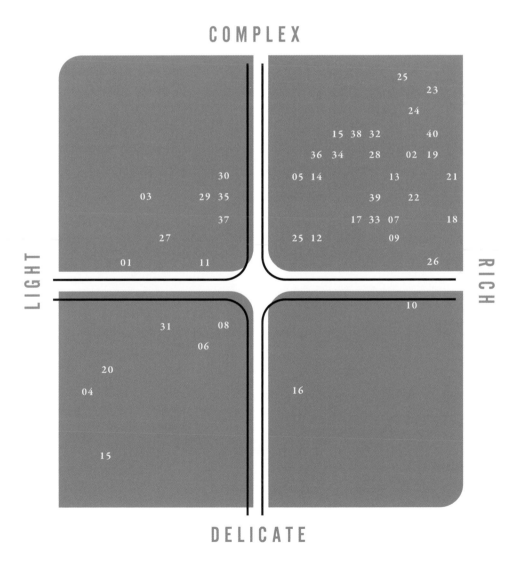

FLAVOR WHEELS BY MATURATION

The wheels also show different flavor profiles based on the type of cask used in maturation. Once you've identified specific flavors, you can then pair and use them to create original and, most importantly, well-balanced balanced drinks.

OK, so you've got a great whiskey.

Naturally, you want to showcase it in a new cocktail. How do you get the best out of it? Trust these wheels . . .

Start with finding the maturation of your whiskey. Which wheels feature that? Look at the flavors that match your whiskey. From this point you can start to assemble the ingredients for a recipe—before you even open your bottle.

Of course, the drink you make may not be perfect first time; it rarely is. However, you'll have the most important thing: a rock-solid starting point. With that, you can finetune the other layers and ingredients as you develop your totally original and absolute killer new drink.

EX-BOURBON — American Barrel / American Oak / 200 Ltrs

OLOROSO SHERRY — American Barrel / American Oak / 200 Ltrs

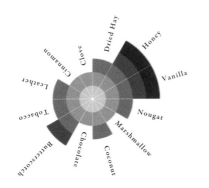

CHESTNUT — American Barrel / American Oak / 200 Ltrs

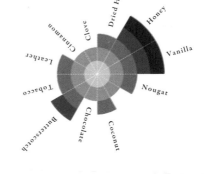

STOUT CASK — American Barrel / American Oak / 200 Ltrs

MADEIRA — American Barrel / American Oak / 200 Ltrs

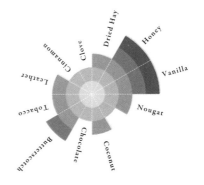

MUSCATEL — American Barrel / American Oak / 200 Ltrs

PORT   American Barrel
American Oak
200 Ltrs

**PEDRO XIMENEZ
/MALAGA WINE**   American Barrel
American Oak
200 Ltrs

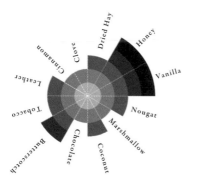

MALAGA   American Barrel
American Oak
200 Ltrs

IPA CASK   American Barrel
American Oak
200 Ltrs

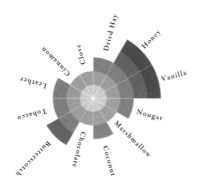

ZINFANDEL   American Barrel
American Oak
200 Ltrs

SAUTERNES   American Barrel
American Oak
200 Ltrs

MARASLA American Barrel
American Oak
200 Ltrs

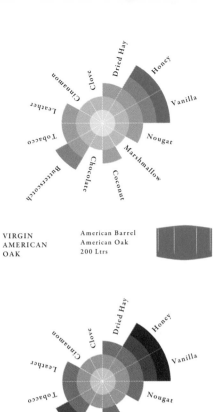

VIRGIN
AMERICAN
OAK
American Barrel
American Oak
200 Ltrs

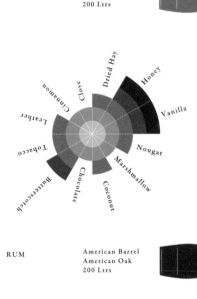

RUM American Barrel
American Oak
200 Ltrs

CALVADOS American Barrel
American Oak
200 Ltrs

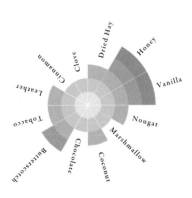

PINEAU DES
CHARENTES
American Barrel
American Oak
200 Ltrs

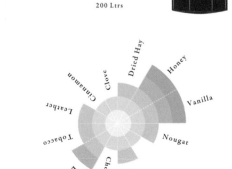

AMBRUANA American Barrel
American Oak
200 Ltrs

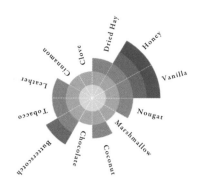

VIRGIN IRISH OAK

American Barrel
American Oak
200 Ltrs

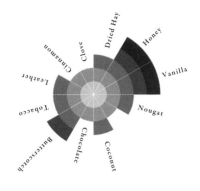

VIRGIN HUNGARIAN OAK

American Barrel
American Oak
200 Ltrs

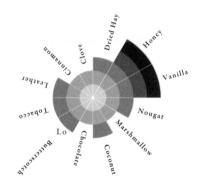

RED BURGUNDY

American Barrel
American Oak
200 Ltrs

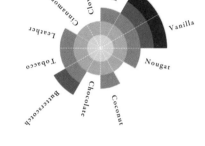

JAPANEESE OAK

American Barrel
American Oak
200 Ltrs

ACACIA

American Barrel
American Oak
200 Ltrs

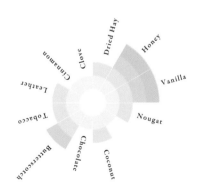

WHITE BURGUNDY

American Barrel
American Oak
200 Ltrs

TASTING IRISH WHISKEY

by Jillian Vose

When tasting and analyzing any spirit, I always approach it afresh and with an open mind—even if I've tasted it a hundred times. It's important to tell yourself that the way you perceive a spirit is sometimes going to be different from how someone else perceives it, and that's OK. There are no shortcuts to becoming a great taster. You need practice, and lots of it. But with that comes a vocabulary that will give you the confidence to consistently describe what you're smelling and tasting.

Tasting and understanding the base spirits you're using plays a key role in creating cocktails. The more you learn about them, the more you'll know when to use one style for certain drinks and when to use another. That is one of the key reasons we're writing this book: to inspire you to use Irish whiskey in more cocktails and to understand the extraordinary versatility within the category.

On the following pages, you'll find tasting notes for bottles we use a lot at the Dead Rabbit. These are a good starting point for you to get out there and taste for yourself. Even if you don't taste the exact same flavors, I'm sure they'll be in the same realm as the descriptors we've listed. The flavor wheels (see page 48) can also help as a guide to get your brain motivated to find the right language to describe what you're smelling and tasting based on the maturation(s) used in the particular whiskey you're analyzing. Though a great deal of tasting is very personal, there are certain things you should be able to pick out of whiskeys based on the raw ingredients (the grain type) and the wood(s) used in maturation.

We hope these tools are helpful to you!

FLAVOR CHARACTERISTICS OF IRISH WHISKEY TYPES AND BOTTLINGS

Here we've broken down the analysis of each whiskey into two main parts: its aroma (or nose) and its palate (or taste). You'll see that there is a great deal of variation within any given style. For completeness, we've also listed the type of maturation the whiskey has undergone.

SINGLE GRAIN

KILBEGGAN

MATURATION: ex-bourbon

AROMA: grassy, wet stone/minerality, acidic, hay, peach, apple, fresh lemon

PALATE: cereal, heather, honey, caramel, toasted oak, vanilla, crème brûlée

TEELING

MATURATION: ex-Cabernet Sauvignon

AROMA: ripe strawberry, fresh nectarine, peach, stone fruit, apple, apricot

PALATE: rich in body, chewy, chocolate orange, marmalade, lots of fruitlike aroma

METHOD AND MADNESS

MATURATION: ex-bourbon (first fill)

AROMA: apricot pit, vanilla, honey glaze, dried oats, dried lemon; virgin oak is very apparent on the nose and there is also a certain dryness or "dustiness"

PALATE: dry, tea biscuity (not scones), oily, candied orange, grainy

THE BUSKER SINGLE GRAIN

MATURATION: ex-bourbon and Marsala cask

AROMA: candied lemon, popcorn, vanilla, cinnamon, dried banana

PALATE: wood tones/oak, banana, baking spice

EGAN'S VINTAGE GRAIN

MATURATION: ex-bourbon cask

AROMA: vanilla, caramel

PALATE: complex

GLENDALOUGH DOUBLE BARREL

MATURATION: ex-bourbon and oloroso sherry

AROMA: vanilla bean, chocolate, baked apple, biscotti, salted butter, blackberry

PALATE: caramel, toasted oak, custard, salt, candied orange, blackberry, black currant, crème brûlée, marzipan, chocolate fudge

CLONAKILTY

MATURATION: Bordeaux cask

AROMA: toasted oak, red berries

PALATE: strawberry, honey, vanilla, toasted wood, black pepper

BALLYHOO (CONNACHT DISTILLERY)

MATURATION: ex-bourbon, port cask finish

AROMA: caramel, rosebud, banana peel, nuts

PALATE: brown sugar, vanilla, floral, mushroom

SINGLE MALTS

KNAPPOGUE CASTLE 12

MATURATION: ex-bourbon

AROMA: peach gummies, pear drops, dried apricot, candied green apple, melon balls, hay, grain, brioche, oaked chardonnay, cashew nut

PALATE: yuzu, dry, white pepper, cocoa nib, stone fruit, baking spice

BUSHMILLS 10

MATURATION: ex-bourbon and sherry

AROMA: Honeycrisp apple, lemon, nougat, peanut, lemongrass, spearmint, honey, vanilla

PALATE: bold orchard fruit, mild floral note, apple, pear, lemon, crème brûlée, brioche, toasted malt

CONNEMARA

MATURATION: ex-bourbon

AROMA: peat smoke, iodine, almond, stone fruit, leather, gasoline, bonfire, peach, raspberry, tar

PALATE: honeycomb, smoke/peat, peach, strawberry jam, turf, wet leaves, seaweed, cinnamon, nutmeg, pumpkin spice

EGAN'S FORTITUDE

MATURATION: Pedro Ximenez sherry

AROMA: prunes, raisin, sherry, tannin, chocolate, honey, marzipan

PALATE: smoke, sweet chocolate, dried fruit, orange peel

THE SEXTON

MATURATION: ex-bourbon and oloroso sherry

AROMA: mince pie, Christmas cake, marzipan, dried cherry, raisin, blanched almond

PALATE: bitter dark chocolate, marmalade, dried berries, blueberry, dark cherry, leather, tobacco

TYRCONNELL 10 PORT CASK

MATURATION: ex-bourbon and port

AROMA: prune, strawberry, Bing cherry, coffee, chocolate, chicory, Brazil nut

PALATE: ripe strawberry, grain, chocolate-covered plum, cherry, apple pie, fig, cinnamon

TULLAMORE D.E.W. 14

MATURATION: ex-bourbon, port, Madeira, and oloroso sherry

AROMA: water chestnut, fresh blueberry, grilled pineapple, pine, Meyer lemon

PALATE: walnut, tangerine, mango, cashew, hazelnut, chicory, chocolate, Heath bar, blackberry, black pepper, Asian pear

WEST CORK GLENGARRIFF BOG OAK CHARRED CASK

MATURATION: charred bog oak casks (Irish oak)

AROMA: smoke, papaya, grilled pineapple, plum, orange, green apple

PALATE: grilled peach, sweet malt, rye bread, plum, orange, leather, earth (like wet leaves, wet stone)

WEST CORK GLENGARRIFF PEATED CHAR CASK SINGLE MALT

MATURATION: sherry cask, ex-bourbon charred with peat

AROMA: cocoa powder, banana, peat, smoke, caramel, BBQ, candied orange

PALATE: toasted malt, grilled pineapple, char, chocolate

THE BUSKER SINGLE MALT

MATURATION: ex-bourbon and ex-sherry

AROMA: dried apricot, cereal grain, honey, lemon, ripe strawberry, white chocolate

PALATE: baked apple, malt, biscotti, pine, chocolate

POT STILL

KNAPPOGUE CASTLE 12

MATURATION: virgin oak, ex-bourbon, and ex-oloroso sherry

AROMA: hay, honey, pencil shavings, earthy, wet stone (virgin oak), banana nut bread, walnut, maple, old leather book, Werther's Original caramel candy

PALATE: ginger, lemon verbena, grainy, spicy, vibrant, cereal grain, honey, cashew

REDBREAST 12

MATURATION: ex-bourbon and oloroso sherry

AROMA: raisin, Christmas cake, walnut, marzipan, tangerine, really ripe strawberry, blackberry jam, banana bread, plum, ripe pear

PALATE: bitter chocolate, orange, very long finish, pomegranate pith, spice, honey-nut cereal

REDBREAST LUSTAU EDITION

MATURATION: ex-bourbon and oloroso sherry

AROMA: ripe plum, toasted walnut or bag of nuts, brown sugar, brown bread, saltwater caramel

PALATE: sticky toffee pudding, plum, ginger, burnt orange, marmalade, nutmeg, toasted oak, peppery, warm baking spices (nutmeg, cinnamon, and clove)

POWERS THREE SWALLOW

MATURATION: ex-bourbon and oloroso sherry

AROMA: cinnamon, nutmeg, mushroom, malty, Brazil nut (skin on), almond, honey, toffee, milk chocolate

PALATE: sherry, sharp berries (like cranberries/blackberries/raspberries), grain-forward, dried date, creamy, linseed, sharp, acid

POWERS JOHN'S LANE

MATURATION: ex-bourbon and oloroso sherry

AROMA: mulled sherry, baking spice, grain-forward, licorice, fennel, nutmeg, strawberry

PALATE: lots of spice, nutmeg-heavy, cinnamon, toffee, rich and bold, dried mango, peach gummies

GREEN SPOT

MATURATION: ex-bourbon and sherry

AROMA: green apple, minty, eucalyptus, caramel, brioche, rosebud

PALATE: a lot of spice on the nose, cinnamon, iodine, buttery, thyme, green, juicy Bartlett pear, green tea/matcha, lemon

YELLOW SPOT

MATURATION: ex-Malaga wine

AROMA: white wine, green grape, dried apricot, white raisin, white chocolate, dried eucalyptus

PALATE: clementine, milk chocolate, lavender, mellow, mild creaminess, Chardonnay, very dry, mild baking spice

THE BUSKER SINGLE POT STILL

MATURATION: ex-bourbon, ex-sherry

AROMA: blueberry jam, fresh flowers, milk chocolate, toffee, black pepper, nuts

PALATE: malt, chocolate, vanilla, lemon oil

DRUMSHANBO

MATURATION: ex-bourbon, ex-sherry

AROMA: vanilla, honey granola, spice cake, chocolate, toasted hazelnut, apricot, char, dried orange peel

PALATE: spice cake, golden raisin, fig, toffee, Nutella, raisin

BLENDS

We finish with blends because hopefully, you've learned about the components first and can therefore better understand the blends. Where we can, we've given at least a rough percentage of each component in the blends.

BUSHMILLS
(SINGLE MALT AND GRAIN WHISKEYS)

MATURATION: five years in ex-bourbon and sherry casks

AROMA: oatmeal cookies with raisins, vanilla, peach, banana

PALATE: caramel, honey, dried pineapple, toasted cereal, malt

BUSHMILLS BLACK BUSH

MATURATION: ex-bourbon and sherry casks

AROMA: apple pie, nutmeg, cinnamon, tannic red wine, fermented strawberry, blackberry, elderflower, cedar, cigar, tangerine

PALATE: cloves, anise, vanilla, toasted brioche, bananas Foster, toasted oak, toasted coconut

DEAD RABBIT

MATURATION: ex-bourbon casks for 5 years; finished for 6 weeks in virgin American oak

AROMA: dried apricot, orange, lemon, damp earth, white truffle, almond, raw coconut

PALATE: nutmeg, white peppery spice, toasted malt, orange, peach/nectarine

JAMESON BLACK BARREL

MATURATION: ex-bourbon casks, re-charred

AROMA: toffee, chicory, toasted coconut, vanilla, smoke, guava

PALATE: cinnamon and clove, vanilla, ripe peach, plantain, dried flowers, black tea

TULLAMORE D.E.W. CARIBBEAN RUM CASK FINISH (POT STILL, SINGLE MALT, AND GRAIN WHISKEYS)

MATURATION: ex-bourbon barrels; finished in Demerara rum casks

AROMA: dried mango, orange, marshmallow, brown sugar, mild baking spices (cinnamon and nutmeg), vanilla, dark cherry

PALATE: banana bread, almond, milk chocolate, baked apple, orange marmalade

POWERS GOLD LABEL

MATURATION: ex-bourbon

AROMA: ripe Anjou pear, lime leaf, honeysuckle, candied orange (orange Tic Tacs, to be precise), eucalyptus, biscotti, lemon curds

PALATE: creamy/rich, honeycomb, toasted cereal, milk chocolate

SLANE

MATURATION: triple casks—virgin oak, ex-bourbon, and ex-sherry

AROMA: caramel, ginger, toasted malt, marzipan, orange, butterscotch

PALATE: dried berries, raisin, hibiscus, blueberry compote

TEELING SMALL BATCH (SINGLE MALT AND GRAIN WHISKEYS)

MATURATION: ex-bourbon; finished in ex-rum barrels

AROMA: toasted chestnut, walnut, thyme, grass, vanilla

PALATE: honey, eucalyptus, hay, heather, candied pineapple, lemon meringue

ROE & CO
(MALT AND GRAIN WHISKEYS)

MATURATION: ex-bourbon

AROMA: heather, honey, lemon peel, vanilla

PALATE: caramel, ginger, lemon, pear

THE BUSKER

MATURATION: ex-bourbon, oloroso Sherry, Marsala casks

AROMA: plum, raisin, banana, pear, vanilla, custard

PALATE: vanilla, dark chocolate, raisin, cinnamon, toasted oak

CLONAKILTY

MATURATION: ex-bourbon, Port finish

AROMA: peach, pie, brown sugar, vanilla, red apple

PALATE: dried berries, cherry, cinnamon, clove, cardamom, chili

DUBLINER

MATURATION: ex-bourbon cask

AROMA: red apple, melted butter, toffee, pear, grass

PALATE: baking spice, smoke, cocoa, charred oak, malt, white pepper

DUBLIN LIBERTIES 'EVIL OAK'

MATURATION: ex-bourbon cask

AROMA: baking spice, golden raisin, vanilla, pepper

PALATE: milk chocolate, burnt malt, pepper, toffee, vanilla, cinnamon, clove, leather

DUNVILLE'S 1808

MATURATION: ex-bourbon

AROMA: vanilla, apple, pear, lemon curd, clean malt

PALATE: ripe citrus, fresh biscuits, white pepper, dry smoke, char

HINCH 'THE ORIGINAL'

MATURATION: ex-bourbon

AROMA: orange marmalade, dried apricot, malt, early, toast, butter

PALATE: chocolate, almond, shortbread, maple, manuka honey, cantaloupe, citrus

HINCH 5-YEAR-OLD DOUBLE WOOD

MATURATION: ex-bourbon, Virgin American Oak

AROMA: smoke, custard, citrus, cream, tobacco

PALATE: peach, mocha, black pepper, honeycomb, chocolate, melon

KILBEGGAN

MATURATION: ex-bourbon

AROMA: caramel, vanilla, oak, pine cone, chestnut, orange, fresh bread

PALATE: kernel corn, hazelnut, cinnamon, cereal grain, pepper, juicy fruit

KILBEGGAN RYE

MATURATION: ex-bourbon

AROMA: Portuguese bread, apple peel, fresh grass, ginger, allspice, cardamom, rye, Asian pear

PALATE: baking spice, caraway, vanilla

PEARSE LYONS 'THE ORIGINAL'

MATURATION: ex-bourbon

AROMA: citrus, smoke, honey, bright fruit, floral

PALATE: spearmint, dark chocolate, light oak, custard, vanilla

PEARSE LYONS 5-YEAR-OLD

MATURATION: ex-bourbon

AROMA: malt, fresh oak, zesty citrus fruit, biscotti, golden raisin

PALATE: sweet malt, pepper spice, candied apple, clove, vanilla, toasted oak

TEELING BLACKPITTS

MATURATION: ex-bourbon, Sauternes

AROMA: smoked BBQ, honeysuckle, bright fruit, orange peel, butterscotch

PALATE: applewood smoke, honey, pear, grilled pineapple, salted caramel

GREEN SPOT
SINGLE POT STILL 40%

Unusually, this triple-distilled 100% pot still contains a cut of the heavier 'hearts' from the distillation process. It is matured in ex-bourbon and in ex-oloroso sherry casks, and the palate offers hints of tropical fruit, pineapple and honey.

WORTH KNOWING
The Spot range began with Mitchell & Son, one of Ireland's oldest whiskey bonders.

POWERS THREE SWALLOWS
SINGLE POT STILL 43.2%, NCF

A triple-distilled, 100% single pot still whiskey, mainly matured in ex-bourbon barrels but subtly finished in former oloroso sherry casks. A sip should reveal hints of tropical fruit, bananas and raisins.

WORTH KNOWING
A revival of the classic style made at the old Dublin distillery.

REDBREAST 12
SINGLE POT S

A triple-distilled, Midleton, 75% matured in 25% in ex-sherry casks in to fading, with some and bananas

WORTH KN
The redbreast name early 1900s by the an and bird

PUTTING IT ALL TOGETHER: WORKING WITH THE DIFFERENT STYLES OF WHISKEY

The three component styles and four distinct categories make Irish whiskey one of the most versatile and adaptable spirit categories. Let's take a look at the characteristics of each category, and what makes them shine in a cocktail.

SINGLE POT STILL

Pot still is a heavier, almost viscous style of whiskey, rich and creamy tasting, resulting from the use of unmalted barley and distillation in a copper pot still. In practice—and for our purposes here—this means it can stand up well to other strong or intense ingredients.

There are two distinct styles of single pot still currently on the market, both of which are produced at Midleton Distillery: spirit-driven and wood-driven. In the former, the flavor profile is largely created by the distillate rather than the aging. With the latter, it is the maturation program that makes the greatest contribution to the final whiskey.

For spirit-driven bottlings such as Powers Signature Release or Powers John's Lane 12, the flavor and body of the whiskey are a great canvas for other flavors. For more sherry-forward, wood-driven pot stills, like the Redbreast expressions or the Spot series, the dried fruit and nuttiness play well with other confectionery flavors as well as tropical fruits.

FOR STIRRED DRINKS, THIS STYLE OF WHISKEY GOES GREAT WITH:

- aromatic bitters
- dark rum
- banana
- chocolate
- celery
- aquavit

FOR CITRUSY DRINKS:

- mango
- fig
- raspberry
- port
- cinnamon
- coconut
- cream

To create original Irish whiskey cocktails, you have to know what the specific flavor characteristics of a given whiskey are. That's where a device like the flavor wheel (see page 48) is very useful.

For example, consider Redbreast 12 here. A quarter of its whiskey is matured in oloroso sherry casks—which is a lot for a single pot still. The other 75 percent is matured in ex-bourbon casks. So, if you look at the wheel, you'll see what flavor you should be pulling from that particular whiskey.

SINGLE MALT

Some people would call it blasphemy to add anything to a single malt, insisting it should just be enjoyed neat. We say, the better the whiskey, the better the drink.

You can gauge what a single malt will contribute to a cocktail based on the casks it was aged in. Ex-bourbon and sherry casks are the most common barrel choices, of course, but there is a lot of innovation in barrel aging these days. There are two distinct styles of single malt: double-distilled and triple-distilled. Double-distilled single malt is extensively produced at the Cooley distillery, with small amounts also made at Kilbeggan and some other distilleries. The liquid tends to showcase the influence of peat, and has a rich, viscous mouthfeel.

The tripled-distilled version is the style for which Bushmills is renowned, and it is dominated by citrus and floral notes. The extra distillation also tends to create a lighter spirit. With wood maturation, additional notes are added, such as fruitcake and dried fruits from ex-oloroso barrels, chocolate and cherries from port casks, and vanilla and aromatic spice from ex-bourbon barrels. These flavors can be further amplified or accentuated by other ingredients when the whiskey is used as the base of a cocktail.

FOR STIRRED DRINKS, THIS STYLE OF WHISKEY GOES GREAT WITH (BUT IS NOT RESTRICTED TO, OF COURSE):

- pear
- peach
- lighter-style vermouths
- Manzanilla and fino sherries
- fruit brandies (young and aged and unaged)
- berries

FOR CITRUSY DRINKS:

- melon (cantaloupe especially)
- almond
- gold rum
- vanilla
- honey
- fig
- cardamom

SINGLE GRAIN

Single grain is probably the least commonly seen Irish whiskey on the market. Right now, there are only a few—but, we hope there are more to come soon. It's very versatile (and excellent on its own).

Grain whiskey makes up a lot of the volume in blended whiskeys, so don't underestimate their quality. They may be on the lighter side, but that's the beauty of them. Single grains are also a great canvas for infusions. They work very well in shaken drinks such as sours, fizzes, Collins, and highballs. The lighter style of spirit that results from column distillation interacts nicely with citrus, bright fruit, herbs, and flowers, and sits really well behind those main flavors.

They can also be used similarly to lighter spirits such as unaged or lightly aged rums, tequilas, and young brandies. Single grain whiskeys tend not to dominate a cocktail, so they offer a perfect stepping-stone into the category for Irish whiskey novices. These categories can also work in cocktails that call for a lighter spirit base, and can soften and lighten bolder modifying agents.

FOR STIRRED DRINKS, THINK OF:

- lighter-style vermouths
- Manzanilla and fino sherries
- lighter sweet vermouths like Cocchi Vermouth di Torino
- smoky or peated whiskeys (to complement the lighter grain and give more complexity)
- apple brandy
- fennel

AND FOR SHAKEN DRINKS:

- blackberry
- peach/nectarine
- orange
- fig
- cucumber
- tomato

BLENDED

This category can be complicated, but it's also the most fun—and there's so much to choose from. Now that you understand all the components, you can decide which blends to use for your drinks based on the raw ingredients and maturation. For instance, with a heavier pot still component, it can stand up to more intense mixers like amaros, heavier vermouths, other strong spirits, etc. With blends featuring lighter whiskeys, typically you want to use lighter modifiers. Because there are so many options in this category, you really need to think about the components within the blends. Therefore, we can't really direct you on flavors as a whole, as there's a blended whiskey for every flavor combination out there. But we have listed some ingredients that have worked well for us.

We've especially had luck with blends due to their versatility and also their price points, for the most part. Shaken drinks are where you'll see blended Irish whiskey used most in our cocktails.

FOR SHAKEN DRINKS, CONSIDER:

- citrus
- ginger/mace
- herbs
- spice
- bitters

- amontillado and oloroso sherries
- aged brandies
- light amari
- vanilla
- apple

THE PRACTICALS

Glassware, Bar Tools, Methods and Techniques, Garnishes

GLASSWARE

First, the bad news. Using the right glass does make a difference. Really. And why is that? Because science. For example, if you serve a cold drink without ice, use a stemmed glass and the drink won't be warmed by the heat of your hand. If the drink has a lot of bubbles, like Champagne, a tall, narrow glass will retain the effervescence longer. And so on. (Plus, in any case, using the right glass shows an extra level of care and attention—which is always good, right?)

So, it's worth the effort. The good news is you can usually get by with what you have—but just for now, OK? Promise you'll definitely get the right ones, yes?

Here are the ones we use in the bar.

- OLD FASHIONED GLASS (12½ OUNCES): a short, squat, heavy-bottomed tumbler with straight sides

- SOUR GLASS (6½ OUNCES): a stemmed cuplike glass similar to a white wine glass, only smaller

- NICK & NORA GLASS (5 OUNCES): a bell-shaped glass with a stem—a bit like an elongated wineglass

- FANCY NICK & NORA GLASS (4¾ OUNCES): like a regular Nick & Nora, but a little smaller and, well, fancier

- HOT TODDY GLASS (6¾ OUNCES): a stemmed Georgian glass larger than an Irish coffee glass

- IRISH COFFEE GLASS (6 OUNCES): we recommend using our own version—naturally—but in any case, make sure it's a relatively thick glass with a good stem

- HIGHBALL OR COLLINS GLASS (11¾ OUNCES): a tall, straight-sided glass with a fairly narrow neck

- TAPROOM HIGHBALL GLASS (12¼ OUNCES): as above in shape, but slightly smaller

- FIZZ GLASS (9 OUNCES): a tall, skinny, straight-sided glass

- FANCY WINEGLASS (12 OUNCES): a short-stemmed all-purpose wineglass

- SINGLE ROCKS GLASS (9¾ OUNCES): similar to an Old Fashioned, but noticeably smaller in volume; most commonly used for Sazerac-style drinks and straight spirits

- COUPETTE OR SMASH GLASS (8 OUNCES): another stemmed glass, like a shallow cocktail glass but with straight sides

- FANCY SOUR OR PUNCH GLASS (8 OUNCES): a stemmed tulip-style sour glass with a wide mouth

- CHAMPAGNE FLUTE (8 OUNCES): a stemmed glass with a narrow neck and mouth, most suitable for sparkling wine cocktails

- BELGIAN TULIP BEER GLASS (16 OUNCES): short-stemmed, bulbous-based glass with a flared tulip mouth

- CONTOURED FIZZ GLASS (10 OUNCES): a tall, long glass with a base and a mouth that contours inward

BAR TOOLS

This book isn't about teaching you how to become a professional bartender. We just want to explain how to make the drinks correctly, so you'll enjoy them more. That's a little easier if you have the right tools to work with. As with the glassware, you can sort of get by without some of these (up to a point), but your drinks will be much better if you're able to measure, extract, shake, strain, and grate your ingredients properly.

Tools you'll need:

- JIGGERS: ¼ ounce, ½ ounce, ¾ ounce, 1 ounce, 2 ounce (yip, you'll use them all)

- BARSPOON: the long spiral handle helps the bowl of the spoon swirl and spin in the glass, saving you effort

- ½-TEASPOON AND 1-TEASPOON MEASURES: again, you'll need both

- STRAINERS: julep (like a large perforated spoon), Hawthorne (the one with the spring thingy), and fine (it's, yes, fine)

- SHAKER TINS: you'll need 18-ounce and 28- to 30-ounce versions

- MIXING GLASS: looks like a tall, wide glass beaker, with a lip for pouring

- ICE PICK: very efficient; plus, they look a bit scary (bonus)

- NUTMEG GRATER: a proper one, mind, not a Microplane

- SOUS VIDE: French for "under vacuum," it is a technique where food, or in this case, syrups and infusions, are placed in a plastic bag, vacuum sealed, and then placed in a water bath at a particular temperature for a particular time. This is a long process of cooking, but it captures flavors in their most honest form, as opposed to direct heat, which adds in most cases a caramelization flavor.

METHODS AND TECHNIQUES

STIR

The point of stirring a drink is to get it cold and diluted to a pleasant balance.

- Build the drink in a mixing glass in the order the recipe indicates.

- Add ice.

- Use a barspoon and stir the drink until it's very cold.

SHAKE

Shaking a drink incorporates air, giving the drink texture. When shaken correctly, the drink should have a fine froth on top and be very cold the whole way through.

- Build the drink in the smaller of the shaker tins in the order the recipe indicates.

- Add ice to fill the tin to the top.

- Drop the larger tin over the smaller tin. Tap to seal them together.

- Pick up the tins and flip them over so your dominant hand is at the top of the smaller tin and your other hand is at the bottom of the larger shaker tin.

- Shake the drink vigorously toward your ear and then away from your body. (Imagine the ice inside moving in a circular motion.)

SHORT SHAKE

A short shake means exactly what it means. You're simply mixing the ingredients up and getting it a bit cold. This technique is mostly used for drinks going over crushed ice or highball-style drinks.

WHIP SHAKE

You will typically whip shake a drink that is being served over cracked ice or with pebble ice.

- Build the drink in the small tin in the order the recipe indicates.

- Add a handful of pebble ice—roughly 15 pieces (or crushed ice, if that's all you have).

- Drop the larger tin over the smaller tin. Tap to seal them together.

- Shake in a whipping motion until the ice has completely melted and you can't hear it anymore.

DRY SHAKE

This is a method used when there is an egg component involved. Always use the freshest eggs you can find—it will make for a much better froth.

- Build the drink in the small tin in the order the recipe indicates.

- Crack an egg into the larger tin.

- Drop the larger tin over the smaller tin (do not add ice). Tap to seal them together.

- Whip shake for 20 to 30 seconds.

- Break the seal to open the tins and add ice to fill the small tin to the top.

- Reseal and shake it longer than usual (to get the texture right).

DOUBLE STRAINING

Double straining means using a Hawthorne strainer to keep the ice back in your shaker tin while simultaneously pouring the liquid through a mesh strainer. This keeps the ice chips or any solid ingredients that were in the tin from getting into the drink.

GARNISHES

We take a fairly minimal approach to garnishes. We reckon that if a garnish doesn't genuinely enhance the drink, it doesn't belong in the glass.

NUTMEG: We find this works really well in our shaken drinks. Be sure to use a proper nutmeg grater. A Microplane will grate chunks of nutmeg rather than a fine dust, which is what you want.

CITRUS OILS: We recommend cutting large, coin-shaped swaths from the fruit, being sure not to get the flesh of the fruit. You only want the oil from the skin. Once you've poured the drink, take the citrus coin and hold it about 5 inches above the glass, with the skin facing down toward the drink. With your thumb and index finger, pinch the coin. This will express the oil onto your drink, giving it a beautiful aromatic note.

AND A WORD OR TWO ABOUT ICE: Yes, it's a detail; but again, it does matter. A single large rock will keep your drink cold and dilute it slower, while more pieces of ice mean faster dilution—the more surface area of ice that touches the liquid, the faster the ice will melt. So keep in mind the type of ice you're using for shaking, stirring, and serving your drinks over. Also, if you use ice to chill the drink while you're mixing it, ideally use fresh ice when you serve it.

IRISH WHISKEY COCKTAILS

by Jillian Vose

While there are few classic cocktails that call specifically for Irish whiskey, it's an extremely mixable spirit in all its forms. Here are some Dead Rabbit versions of those classics that illustrate the point. Then, in the following section, you'll find some of the many original drinks we've created that truly showcase the variety of the spirit.

We've not only given the exact ingredients for each drink—highlighting the key whiskey involved—but also listed the bar tools to use, the method for assembling the drink, and even the garnish for that all-important finishing touch. Even if you're not very experienced in making drinks like this, we think you'll find these recipes unique and inspiring, and relatively easy to follow. Take your time, persevere, and the reward will be there in the glass.

You'll find details of how to make any bespoke ingredients mentioned here in the Syrups, Tinctures, and Infusions section starting on page 239.

CLASSIC IRISH WHISKEY COCKTAILS

IRISH COFFEE

sweet, creamy, delicate

Adapted by Dale DeGroff and Jillian Vose

INGREDIENTS

1 ounce Bushmills The Original

⅝ ounce demerara syrup (page 251)

3½ ounces brewed Sumatra Mandheling filtered coffee, hot

Heavy cream

GARNISH: Nutmeg, for grating (optional)

TOOLS

Coffee maker, jigger, nutmeg grater (optional)

GLASSWARE

6-ounce Irish coffee glass

METHOD

Add the whiskey, demerara syrup, and hot coffee to an Irish coffee glass. Stir to ensure the syrup is evenly distributed. Leave a finger's worth of room for whipped cream. Top with freshly whipped cream and garnish with freshly grated nutmeg, if you wish.

This is one of the most iconic, beloved, and misunderstood cocktails of all. We spent years perfecting the method and finessing every variation of this simple four-ingredient recipe. It's become our signature drink, enjoyed and lovingly recalled by visitors from around the world.

FEATURED WHISKEY

Bushmills The Original blended Irish whiskey

With a recipe that dates to before Prohibition, Bushmills The Original is the flagship whiskey from the world's oldest licensed whiskey distillery. The master distiller has an original bottle from the year 1888 that he sips from time to time to ensure the quality of the liquid has been maintained over the years.

TIPPERARY

rich, balanced, familiar

Adapted by Jack McGarry and Jillian Vose

INGREDIENTS

3 dashes Angostura bitters

3 dashes orange bitters

3 dashes Vieux Pontarlier absinthe

½ ounce green Chartreuse

1½ ounces house sweet vermouth (page 259)

1½ ounces Powers Three Swallow single pot still

GARNISH: Orange peel, for squeezing

TOOLS

Jiggers, mixing glass, barspoon, julep strainer

GLASSWARE

Cocktail glass

METHOD

Add the ingredients to a mixing glass in the order indicated and stir with ice. Strain into a cocktail glass without ice. Garnish with a spritz of orange oil and discard the peel.

This cocktail's first appearance in print was in 1917 in *Recipes for Mixed Drinks* by Hugo R. Ensslin. It was said to be named after a guest walked in asking for a drink while humming "It's a Long Way to Tipperary," an anthem for homesick Irish soldiers during World War I. Other credit is given to Harry Craddock, who included it in his 1930 classic *The Savoy Cocktail Book*.

FEATURED WHISKEY

Powers Three Swallow single pot still Irish whiskey

CAMERON'S KICK

nutty, dry, peat

Adapted by Jack McGarry and Greg Buda

INGREDIENTS

3 dashes Angostura bitters

¾ ounce fresh lemon juice

¾ ounce orgeat (page 265)

¾ ounce Barbadillo oloroso sherry

1 ounce Bowmore 12 peated single malt Scotch

1 ounce Redbreast 12 single pot still

GARNISH: Nutmeg, for grating

TOOLS

Jiggers, shaker tins, fine strainer, Hawthorne strainer, nutmeg grater

GLASSWARE

Coupette

METHOD

Add the ingredients to a shaker tin in the order indicated and shake with ice. Double strain using both the fine and Hawthorne strainers into a coupette and serve with an ice nugget. Garnish with freshly grated nutmeg.

Nobody knows for sure who created this drink—and even fewer know who Cameron was—but what is certain is that it's an exceptional concoction. The original was just a mix of equal parts Scotch and Irish whiskeys, plus lemon and orgeat, to which we've added oloroso sherry and bitters for extra depth and balance.

FEATURED WHISKEY

Redbreast 12-Year-Old single pot still Irish whiskey

EMERALD

aromatic, bold, assertive

Adapted by Jack McGarry and Jillian Vose

INGREDIENTS

2 dashes Angostura bitters

1 teaspoon Pierre Ferrand dry curaçao

1 ounce house sweet vermouth (page 259)

2 ounces Powers Three Swallow single pot still

GARNISH: Lemon and orange twists, for squeezing

TOOLS

Jiggers, mixing glass, barspoon, julep strainer

GLASSWARE

Nick & Nora glass

METHOD

Add the ingredients to a mixing glass in the order indicated and stir together lightly. Strain into a Nick & Nora glass. Garnish with a spritz each of lemon oil and orange oil and discard the peels.

It's been argued—with some vigor—that the Emerald is an Irish version of the classic Manhattan, the rye replaced with Irish whiskey. And like the original Manhattan, it even contains a hint of orange commingled with the fruit of Erin's green isle. Well, we are very adaptable people.

FEATURED WHISKEY

Powers Three Swallow single pot still Irish whiskey

BANKERS PUNCH

rich, fruity, robust

Created by Jack McGarry

INGREDIENTS

3 dashes Angostura bitters

¾ ounce fresh lime juice

¾ ounce raspberry syrup
(see page 267)

¾ ounce W. & J. Graham's late
bottled vintage port

¼ ounce Smith & Cross Jamaica rum

¼ ounce Banks 7 Golden Age rum

¼ ounce Cruzan blackstrap rum

¾ ounce Redbreast 12 single pot still

GARNISH: Nutmeg, for grating

TOOLS

Jiggers, shaker tins, fine strainer,
nutmeg grater

GLASSWARE

Punch glass

METHOD

Add the ingredients to a shaker tin
in the order indicated and shake
with 3 ice cubes. Fine strain into
a punch glass over pebble ice or
crushed ice. Garnish lightly with
freshly grated nutmeg.

Jack rescued and developed this drink from a
couple of almost-forgotten nineteenth-century
cocktails, the Irish Planter's Punch and the
Knickerbocker. The Redbreast supplies spiciness
and complexity and the overproof blend of
rums brings heat and depth, while the port and
fruit elements provide wonderful softness and
sweetness.

FEATURED WHISKEY

Redbreast 12-Year-Old single pot still Irish whiskey

WILD IRISH ROSE

tart, floral, fresh

Adapted by Jack McGarry and Jillian Vose

INGREDIENTS

1 egg white

3 dashes Bittermens Burlesque Bitters

3 dashes Vieux Pontarlier absinthe

¾ ounce fresh lemon juice

¾ ounce grenadine (page 256)

½ ounce Cocchi Americano Rosa

1 ounce Laird's applejack

1 ounce Connemara peated single malt

GARNISH: Lemon peel, for squeezing

TOOLS

Jiggers, shaker tins, fine strainer, Hawthorne strainer

GLASSWARE

Punch glass

METHOD

Add the ingredients to a shaker tin in the order indicated. Dry shake without ice, then shake with ice. Double strain using both the fine and Hawthorne strainers into a punch glass without ice. Garnish with a spritz of lemon oil and discard the peel.

If you look at the original recipe for this drink and compare it with our version, you'll see some differences. But the bones are still there: citrus, grenadine, whiskey. Jack then accentuated the tart and fruity sour with layers of hibiscus, absinthe, floral vermouth, and peated Irish whiskey. It's an all-time favorite at the bar.

FEATURED WHISKEY

Connemara peated single malt Irish whiskey

Inspired by the 18th-century practice of drying malting barley over peat fires, Connemara possesses a warming peaty flavor and aroma, instilling a delicate smokiness and smooth, sweet taste and has helped to inspire a rekindled interest in the production of peated Irish whiskies.

DEAD RABBIT ORIGINAL IRISH WHISKEY COCKTAILS

These are original cocktails we've created around the distinctive characteristics and flavors of the various styles of Irish whiskey. In some drinks, we use additional ingredients in order to highlight those particular characteristics, while in other drinks, they supplement the nature of the whiskey, creating an entirely new, complex, and balanced cocktail.

SINGLE GRAIN IRISH WHISKEY COCKTAILS

CHIEF OF STAFF

bright, rosebud, cereal grain

Created by Long Thai

INGREDIENTS

½ teaspoon house maraschino
liqueur (page 258)

½ teaspoon Giffard crème de cacao

¼ ounce palo cortado sherry

¼ ounce Giffard rhubarb liqueur

¾ ounce Martini & Rossi Riserva
Speciale Rubino vermouth

1½ ounces Egan's Fortitude

GARNISH: Lemon peel, for
squeezing

TOOLS

Jiggers, mixing glass, barspoon, julep
strainer

GLASSWARE

Nick & Nora glass

METHOD

Add the ingredients to a mixing glass
in the order indicated and stir with
ice. Strain into a Nick & Nora glass
without ice. Garnish with a spritz of
lemon oil and discard the peel.

Talk about how the bold and subtle can come
together to form something beautifully balanced.
This exclusively PX sherry-aged single malt
whiskey is accented with floral and berry
notes coming together to form a medium-
bodied Manhattan variation. This meets right
in the middle for someone who likes boozy or
refreshing drinks.

FEATURED SINGLE GRAIN

Egan's Fortitude Irish whiskey

DEVIL WOMAN

refreshing, savory, long

Created by Greg Buda

INGREDIENTS

4 dashes black pepper tincture
(page 242)

¾ ounce fresh lime juice

¼ ounce beet syrup (page 240)

½ ounce coffee-pecan syrup
(page 249)

½ ounce blackberry shrub
(page 241)

½ ounce Manzanilla sherry

½ ounce The Famous Grouse Smoky
Black blended Scotch

1½ ounces Kilbeggan single grain

TOOLS

Jiggers, shaker tins, fine strainer,
Hawthorne strainer, ice pick

GLASSWARE

Collins glass

METHOD

Add the ingredients to a shaker tin
in the order indicated and shake
with ice. Double strain using both
the fine and Hawthorne strainers
into a collins glass over cracked ice.

It might seem odd to use a single grain Irish whiskey here among so many powerful other flavors. However, splitting the base with a smoky Scotch mellowed it out and allowed the other ingredients to come through, while keeping the proof level suitably elevated.

FEATURED SINGLE GRAIN

Kilbeggan single grain Irish whiskey

Cooley and the man behind it, John Teeling, have played seminal roles in the revival of the Irish distilling industry in the late 20th century. When it opened in 1989, Cooley was the first new distillery built in Ireland in over a hundred years. Cooley also revived numerous brands including Kilbeggan, Tyrconnell, and Connemara.

ROLLERBALL

fruit, calming, light

Created by Long Thai

INGREDIENTS

3 dashes Dale DeGroff's pimento bitters

¾ ounce fresh lemon juice

½ ounce nectarine juice

¼ ounce fennel syrup (page 254)

¾ ounce raspberry syrup (page 267)

2 ounces Clonakilty Bordeaux cask single grain

GARNISH: Lemon peel, for squeezing

TOOLS

Jiggers, shaker tins, fine strainer, Hawthorne strainer

GLASSWARE

Sour glass

METHOD

Add the ingredients to a shaker tin in the order indicated and shake with ice. Double strain using both the fine and Hawthorne strainers into a sour glass without ice. Garnish with a spritz of lemon oil and discard the peel.

This whiskey is great for mixing because its proof is on the higher side, at 43.6% ABV, and since it's been finished in Bordeaux barrels, there are strong berry and rhubarb notes and a lot of orchard fruit coming from the distillate itself. The flavor pairings are thoughtful and elegantly complement the nose of the whiskey.

FEATURED SINGLE GRAIN

Clonakilty Bordeaux cask single grain Irish whiskey

The Egan family have been involved in Irish whiskey since the 1800s, when Patrick and Henry Egan established general merchants P. & H. Egan Limited in the heart of Tullamore, county Offaly. As well as being merchants, they were also grocers, hoteliers, ironmongers, maltsters, brewers, and bonders. It was said that the Egan's would look after you from the cradle to the grave as they would sell your parents your cot to sleep in, your casket, and everything in between.

TRAILBLAZER

tangy, baking spice, bright

Created by Jillian Vose

INGREDIENTS

1 dash mace tincture (page 261)

⅓ teaspoon cinnamon bark syrup (page 248)

⅓ teaspoon passion fruit syrup (page 265)

⅓ teaspoon Giffard crème de pêche

¾ ounce Martini & Rossi Ambrato vermouth

1½ ounces The Busker single grain

GARNISH: Lemon peel, for squeezing

TOOLS

Teaspoon, jiggers, mixing glass, barspoon, julep strainer

GLASSWARE

Coupe

METHOD

Add the ingredients to a mixing glass in the order indicated and stir with ice. Strain into a coupe glass without ice. Garnish with a spritz of lemon oil and discard the peel. (We suggest batching the ⅓ teaspoons together and then measuring the batched ingredients with 1 teaspoon to add to the mixing glass for accuracy.)

I had the pleasure of working with The Busker on their launch campaign in 2021. It was exciting to see a new line of whiskey that makes all four styles in one house, as it's quite rare. The single grain really stuck out to me as the category has only a few choices and I just couldn't wait to make a drink with it. The accent flavors here, cinnamon and passion fruit, are pairings to the aromas I picked out of the whiskey itself, making a beautiful, elegant, light, and refreshing stirred whiskey cocktail (if I say so myself). It's a balance of many of the things I love in a light stirred drink—approachable, bright, yet boozy and great for any time of the year. I'm definitely proud of this one.

FEATURED SINGLE GRAIN

The Busker single grain Irish whiskey

The Busker single grain is made with wheat and matured in bourbon casks and rare Marsala casks from Cantine Florio 1833, one of the oldest Sicilian wineries. Royal Oak Distillery, the home of The Busker, is the only distillery in Ireland currently making all styles of Irish whiskey—blend, single pot still, single malt, and single grain—under the same roof.

GUILT TRIP

creamy, tangy, fresh

Created by Harrison Ginsberg

INGREDIENTS

1 dash house orange bitters
(page 259)

4 dashes za'atar tincture (page 279)

1 teaspoon Strega

¾ ounce fresh lemon juice

¾ ounce sumac syrup (page 274)

1½ ounces Teeling single grain

1 teaspoon Greek yogurt

GARNISH: Nutmeg, for grating

TOOLS

Shaker tins, jiggers, fine strainer,
Hawthorne strainer, nutmeg grater

GLASSWARE

Sour glass

METHOD

Add the ingredients to a shaker tin
in the order indicated and shake
with ice. Double strain using both
the fine and Hawthorne strainers
into a sour glass without ice. Garnish
lightly with freshly grated nutmeg.

This is a very unusual but wonderful drink,
inspired by Israeli cuisine. Teeling single grain
is not only a great canvas for many flavors and
styles of drinks, but the light tannin that comes
from the barrel can also stand up to this rich and
tangy concoction.

FEATURED SINGLE GRAIN

Teeling single grain Irish whiskey

Teeling whiskey brings new flavors to Irish
whiskey using innovative cask maturation
techniques like its Cabernet Sauvignon-
matured single grain whiskey.

GLOW WORM

baking spice, intense, boozy

Created by Jillian Vose

INGREDIENTS

1 dash The Bitter Truth aromatic bitters

¾ ounce fresh lemon juice

¼ ounce ginger syrup (page 255)

½ ounce fig syrup (page 254)

¼ ounce Dead Rabbit Jamaica rum blend (page 250)

½ ounce Alvear pale cream sherry

2 ounces sesame-infused Kilbeggan single grain (page 270)

GARNISH: Nutmeg, for grating

TOOLS

Jiggers, shaker tins, fine strainer, Hawthorne strainer, nutmeg grater

GLASSWARE

Sour glass

METHOD

Add the ingredients to a shaker tin in the order indicated and shake with ice. Double strain using both the fine and Hawthorne strainers into a sour glass without ice. Garnish lightly with freshly grated nutmeg.

I chose Kilbeggan for this drink because it can stand up to more intense flavors than other single grains and blends. Anything with fresh ginger can sometimes take over a drink, but the toasted sesame infusion used here provides a really great meld of flavors for this spicy sour.

FEATURED SINGLE GRAIN

Kilbeggan single grain Irish whiskey

Founded in 1757, Kilbeggan, the oldest licensed distillery in Ireland, makes delicious and versatile Irish blended whiskey beloved by the world over. When tough times ground its gears to a halt, the town, which it's named after, came together to save the whiskey. Today, every bottle produced stands as proof that the spirit of Kilbeggan never wavered.

TRANSFORMER

hoppy, grain, savory

Created by Jesse Vida

INGREDIENTS

1 dash Bittermens Hopped Grapefruit bitters

1 teaspoon fennel syrup (page 254)

½ ounce fino sherry

¾ ounce Cocchi Americano

¼ ounce Clear Creek Reserve apple brandy

½ ounce unpeated single malt Scotch

1¼ ounces Teeling single grain

TOOLS

Jiggers, mixing glass, barspoon, julep strainer

GLASSWARE

Nick & Nora glass

METHOD

Add the ingredients to a mixing glass in the order indicated and stir with ice. Strain into a Nick & Nora glass without ice and serve.

Teeling single grain is aged exclusively in ex-bourbon barrels and comes with a high ABV of 46%. It's quite cereal grain–forward, with notes of hay, vanilla, caramel, and baking spices within its rich texture. Here it played really nicely with the lighter fortified modifiers, complemented by the apple brandy. The contrast with the hopped grapefruit bitters adds still more layers.

FEATURED SINGLE GRAIN

Teeling single grain Irish whiskey

BARE-FACED LIAR
sour, berry, aromatic

Created by Jillian Vose

INGREDIENTS

Toasted fennel salt (page 276)

2 dashes The Bitter Truth Jerry Thomas' Own Decanter bitters

¾ ounce fresh lemon juice

¼ ounce beet syrup (page 240)

½ ounce raspberry syrup (page 267)

½ ounce Dubonnet Rouge

2 ounces Ballyhoo

TOOLS

Spice grinder, jiggers, shaker tins, fine strainer, Hawthorne strainer

GLASSWARE

Sour glass

METHOD

Rim half the glass with fennel salt. Add the rest of the ingredients in the order indicated to a shaker tin and shake with ice. Double strain using both the fine and Hawthorne strainers into the prepared sour glass without ice.

This came about by experimenting with Connacht's Ballyhoo single grain. Its higher proof and nuances of rosebud and vanilla paired well with the beet and raspberry sweeteners. The nutty and earth tones worked glamorously with the toasted fennel salt garnish. The dubonnet lengthens the drink without over-proofing it or making the drink muddy.

FEATURED SINGLE GRAIN

Ballyhoo Irish whiskey

Connacht is a small, family-owned craft distiller in country Mayo in the west of Ireland focused on producing premium, small-batch whiskeys. It enjoys a unique location between the freshwater rivers and loughs, which feed the distillery, and the maritime climate of the Atlantic, whose influence makes its way into the barrels of whiskey maturing on-site.

GOD IS A DJ

savory, inviting, baking spice

Created by Jillian Vose

INGREDIENTS

2 dashes Dale DeGroff Pimento bitters

1 teaspoon cinnamon bark syrup (page 248)

¾ ounce lemon juice

¼ ounce maple syrup (grade B)

½ ounce banana syrup (page 240)

½ ounce Alvear pale cream sherry

1½ ounces Teeling single grain

GARNISH: Nutmeg, for grating

TOOLS

Jiggers, mixing tins, fine strainer, Hawthorne strainer, nutmeg grater

GLASSWARE

Sour glass

METHOD

Add the ingredients in the order indicated to a shaker tin and shake with ice. Double strain using both the fine and Hawthorne strainers into a sour glass without ice. Garnish with freshly grated nutmeg.

This was a shaken interpretation of another drink, the Gold Digger (page 189). When turning a stirred drink concept into a shaken one, you have to consider the addition of sugar to balance out the citrus. If you compare the two, you'll see that the stirred Gold Digger has a lengthener of Cocchi Americano, whereas here the Cocchi is replaced with more substantial ingredients including banana and maple syrups.

FEATURED SINGLE GRAIN

Teeling single grain Irish whiskey

SINGLE MALT IRISH WHISKEY COCKTAILS

OLD SMOKE

savory, floral, full-bodied

Created by Jack McGarry

INGREDIENTS

3 Dashes Bittermens Orchard Street Celery bitters

3 dashes Vieux Pontarlier absinthe

½ ounce parfait amour liqueur

1½ ounces house sweet vermouth (page 259)

1½ ounces Connemara peated single malt

GARNISH: Orange peel, for squeezing

TOOLS

Jiggers, mixing glass, barspoon, julep strainer

GLASSWARE

Cocktail glass

METHOD

Add the ingredients to a mixing glass in the order indicated and stir with ice. Strain into a cocktail glass without ice. Garnish with a spritz of orange oil and discard the peel.

Celery and absinthe are a no-brainer pairing. Parfait amour is a curaçao-based liqueur with other botanicals and violette. The smoke as a contrasting flavor is perfect, and when creating drinks with it, think outside the box—like Jack did.

FEATURED SINGLE MALT

Connemara peated single malt Irish whiskey

PERFECT STORM

elegant, herbal, fragrant

Created by Jack McGarry

INGREDIENTS

2 dashes Peychaud's bitters

2 dashes Bittermens Boston Bittahs

¼ ounce Dolin Génépy le Chamois

½ ounce Pür Likör Williams pear liqueur

¾ ounce Cocchi Americano

¾ ounce Lemorton Selection Calvados Domfrontais

¾ ounce Knappogue Castle 12 single malt

GARNISH: Lemon peel, for squeezing

TOOLS

Jiggers, mixing glass, barspoon, julep strainer

GLASSWARE

Nick & Nora glass

METHOD

Add the ingredients in the order indicated to a mixing glass and stir with ice. Strain into a Nick & Nora glass without ice. Garnish with a spritz of lemon oil and discard the peel.

This lighter-styled Manhattan variation showcases the apple and pear notes in the elegant and fruity Knappogue single malt, complemented by the herbaceous accents of chamomile, génépy, Cocchi, and bitters.

FEATURED SINGLE MALT

Knappogue Castle 12-Year-Old single malt Irish whiskey

GOOD LUCK CHARM

rich, orange, boozy

Created by Jillian Vose

INGREDIENTS

2 dashes Vieux Pontarlier absinthe

½ ounce Rhum Clément Créole Shrubb

¼ ounce Royal Combier

¾ ounce Amaro Nardini

1½ ounces Bushmills 10 single malt

GARNISH: Orange peel, for squeezing

TOOLS

Jiggers, mixing glass, barspoon, julep strainer

GLASSWARE

Old Fashioned glass

METHOD

Add the ingredients in the order indicated to a mixing glass and stir with ice. Strain into an Old Fashioned glass over a large chunk of ice. Garnish with a spritz of orange oil and discard the peel.

Featuring a full ¾ ounce of amaro, this riff on an Old Fashioned reads very dark and bitter. However, the light and fruity single malt pairs nicely with the anise, kümmel, spices, orange, and bitter notes of the other components and lends balance and complexity.

FEATURED SINGLE MALT

Bushmills 10-Year-Old single malt Irish whiskey

Bushmills 10-Year-Old single malt Irish whiskey is made from 100% malted barley and matured in bourbon and sherry casks. It is a favorite of the first female master blender in the history of Irish whiskey, Bushmills' own Helen Mulholland.

STRONGHOLD

tangy, smoky, robust

Created by Jesse Vida

INGREDIENTS

1 dash Angostura bitters

¾ ounce fresh lemon juice

½ ounce Asian pear juice

½ ounce pistachio orgeat (page 267)

½ ounce Giffard crème de cacao

1½ ounces West Cork Glengarriff peat charred cask finish

GARNISH: Nutmeg, for grating

TOOLS

Jiggers, shaker tins, fine strainer, Hawthorne strainer, ice pick, nutmeg grater

GLASSWARE

Punch glass

METHOD

Add the ingredients to a shaker tin in the order indicated and shake with ice. Double strain using both the fine and Hawthorne strainers into a punch glass and serve with an ice nugget. Garnish with a light dusting of freshly grated nutmeg.

Here Jesse took a simple sour template, combined a beautiful base of complementary sweet and sour modifiers, and used a diverse single malt aged in sherry casks which was finished in charred Irish oak. The whiskey's peated element is sensational against the pistachio and Asian pear.

FEATURED SINGLE MALT

West Cork Glengarriff peat charred cask finish Irish whiskey

Neighboring the distillery's hometown of Skibbereen are the ancient woodlands of the Glengarriff Forest in West Cork. More than six thousand years ago, forests of oak grew where these boglands are today. The remains of those forests are found sunk 15 to 20 feet deep in the bogs, and the oak trees have changed in color to black. Both the peat from the bogland and the oak beneath the bog are harvested.

WATCH TOWER

fragrant, complex, tart

Created by Jillian Vose

INGREDIENTS

1 barspoon Greek yogurt

2 dashes turmeric citrus (page 277)

¾ ounce fresh lemon juice

½ ounce pineapple juice

¾ ounce cinnamon bark syrup
(page 248)

¼ ounce Pierre Ferrand Pineau des
Charentes

¼ ounce Giffard white crème de
cacao

¼ ounce Merlet crème de pêche

1 ounce Bertoux brandy

1 ounce Tyrconnell 10 Madeira cask

GARNISH: Nutmeg, for grating

TOOLS

Jiggers, barspoon, shaker tins, fine
strainer, Hawthorne strainer, nutmeg
grater

GLASSWARE

Punch glass

Bertoux is a blended grape brandy created
expressly for cocktails. It's bright and fresh and
very aromatic, so it's ideal for splitting with other
spirits. Here it pairs wonderfully with the peach,
caramel, and orange notes of the Madeira cask
finish influence in this single malt Irish whiskey
expression. The addition of yogurt tones down
the brightness and adds a little tanginess.

FEATURED SINGLE MALT

Tyrconnell 10-Year-Old Madeira cask Irish whiskey

METHOD

Add the ingredients to a shaker tin in the order
indicated and shake with ice. Double strain using both
the fine and Hawthorne strainers into a punch glass
without ice. Garnish with a light dusting of freshly
grated nutmeg.

In 1876, fortune favored R. M. Delamere
when he entered his chestnut colt,
Tyrconnell, in the prestigious National
Produce Stakes horse race. Tyrconnell,
a 100/1 outsider, bested horses and
oddsmakers alike with a surprise victory.
A. A. Watt, a local gentlemen distiller,
commemorated the occasion by creating a
small-batch whiskey that bore the name of
the unlikely local champion, which became
Watt's most popular whiskey.

LOVE SHACK

coriander, rich, uplifting

Created by Greg Buda

INGREDIENTS

1 egg white

2 dashes Dale DeGroff Pimento bitters

¾ ounce lemon juice

1 ounce sunflower orgeat (page 275)

2 ounces Teeling Blackpitts peated single malt

1½ ounces coriander-infused Glenmorangie 10 (page 249)

¾ ounce half-and-half

Soda water, to top

GARNISH: Orange peel, for squeezing

TOOLS

Jiggers, mixing tins, fine strainer, Hawthorne strainer

GLASSWARE

Fizz glass

Greg based this fizz cocktail around the flavor set of sunflower, coriander, orange, and smoke. The whiskey has sweet grape and honey notes that pair perfectly with the nuttiness and spice components. With the Teeling's ABV being 46%, Greg chose a lengthener of soda water, which allows the whiskey to retain its characteristics against the other elements.

FEATURED SINGLE MALT

Teeling Blackpitts peated single malt Irish whiskey

METHOD

Add the bitters, egg white, lemon juice, sunflower orgeat, half-and-half, infused Glenmorangie, and Teeling to a shaker tin. First dry shake without ice, then shake with ice. Add soda water to the tin. Double strain using both the fine and Hawthorne strainers into a fizz glass without ice. Top with soda until the drink is raised above the rim of the glass. Garnish with a spritz of orange oil and discard the peel.

> With roots in Irish whiskey distillation dating back to 1782, Teeling whiskey's philosophy is to craft with respect for generations passed and have confidence to forge the next chapter. They believe the taste of the future of Irish whiskey is in their rare peated Irish single malt, Blackpitts.

STUN GRENADE
adventurous, tropical, strong

Created by Jillian Vose

INGREDIENTS

1 dash Bitter Truth Jerry Thomas Decanter bitters

1 dash Vicardio dragancello liqueur

½ teaspoon sumac syrup (page 274)

½ teaspoon Giffard Caribbean pineapple liqueur

½ ounce Alvear pale cream sherry

½ ounce Cocchi Storico Vermouth di Torino

1 ounce carrot-infused Plantation 3 Stars white rum (page 244)

1 ounce West Cork 12 rum cask

GARNISH: Orange peel, for squeezing

TOOLS

Jiggers, mixing glass, julep strainer

GLASSWARE

Nick & Nora glass

METHOD

Add the ingredients to a mixing glass in the order indicated and stir with ice. Strain into a Nick & Nora glass without ice. Garnish with a spritz of orange oil and discard the peel.

This drink started as a challenge I set myself. It seemed pretty natural to pair carrot-infused rum with a rum-finished Irish whiskey that had some nice tropical notes and sweetness to it. For more dimension, the chocolaty Cocchi Storico Vermouth di Torino was split with pale cream sherry. Dragoncello brings herby complexity, while the sumac syrup adds a tanginess and texture, and the pineapple liqueur accentuates the rum cask–finished whiskey.

FEATURED SINGLE MALT

West Cork 12-Year-Old rum cask Irish whiskey

SWEAR BLIND

berries, after-dinner, rich

Created by Long Thai

INGREDIENTS

1 egg white

1 dash Angostura bitters

½ ounce maple syrup (grade B)

¾ ounce Giffard crème de banane

1 ounce W. & J. Graham's late bottled vintage port

¾ ounce High West Silver Whiskey Western Oat

1 ounce Egan's Fortitude single malt

GARNISH: Nutmeg, for grating

TOOLS

Jiggers, shaker tins, fine strainer, Hawthorne strainer, nutmeg grater

GLASSWARE

Hot toddy glass

METHOD

Add the ingredients (including the egg) to a shaker tin in the order indicated and shake with ice. Double strain using both the fine and Hawthorne strainers into a toddy glass. Garnish with freshly grated nutmeg.

Two things inspired Long in the creation of this cocktail. The first was discovering the intense flavors in the white whiskey. The second, was a meal—a breakfast dish in this case that included maple syrup, oats, and banana. As he developed this drink he split the base, Egan's Fortitude single malt, which brought out its dried fruit component due to the Pedro Ximenez casks, complementing the other ingredients that evoke Long's wondrous breakfast of legend.

FEATURED SINGLE MALT

Egan's Fortitude single malt Irish whiskey

BROADWAY JUNCTION
bitter, strong, rich

Created by Jillian Vose

INGREDIENTS

1 dash The Bitter Truth Creole bitters

½ ounce Campari

½ ounce Tempus Fugit crème de noyaux

1½ ounces The Sexton single malt

GARNISH: Grapefruit peel, for squeezing

TOOLS

Jiggers, mixing glass, barspoon, julep strainer

GLASSWARE

Old Fashioned glass

METHOD

Add the ingredients to a mixing glass in the order indicated and stir with ice. Strain into an Old Fashioned glass over a large block of ice. Garnish with a spritz of grapefruit oil and discard the peel.

This drink is like a Boulevardier meets a Japanese cocktail with a twist. The Sexton was chosen because it has enough of a backbone to stand up to Campari and rich almond liqueur. It's also exclusively aged in oloroso barrels, giving the drink a strong dried fruit and berry component.

FEATURED SINGLE MALT

The Sexton single malt Irish whiskey

SINGLE POT STILL IRISH WHISKEY COCKTAILS

REVOLVER

complex, grassy, fragrant

Created by Jack McGarry

INGREDIENTS

3 dashes house orange bitters
(page 259)

3 dashes Vieux Pontarlier absinthe

¼ ounce Branca Menta

½ ounce Noilly Prat dry vermouth

½ ounce Avèze gentiane liqueur

¾ ounce green Chartreuse

1½ ounces Teeling single pot still

GARNISH: Lemon peel, for
squeezing

TOOLS

Jiggers, mixing glass, barspoon, julep
strainer

GLASSWARE

Nick & Nora glass

METHOD

Add the ingredients to a mixing glass
in the order indicated and stir with
ice. Strain into a Nick & Nora glass
without ice. Garnish with a spritz of
lemon oil and discard the peel.

This is a light, boozy drink that incorporates
herby, floral notes from the absinthe and
gentiane, while the lightest of pot still Irish
whiskeys contributes orchard fruits and just the
slightest hint of sherry maturation.

FEATURED SINGLE POT STILL

Teeling single pot still Irish whiskey

In 2015, Teeling whiskey proudly opened
the first new distillery in Dublin's city center
in over 125 years. When the company
released the Teeling single pot still it was
the first whiskey distilled in Dublin in nearly
50 years.

THUNDERBOLT

full, decadent, powerful

Created by Jack McGarry

INGREDIENTS

2 dashes Angostura bitters

2 dashes Bittermens Xocolatl Mole bitters

¼ ounce St. Elizabeth allspice dram

½ ounce Domaine de Canton ginger liqueur

½ ounce Giffard crème de banane

1½ ounces Powers John's Lane single pot still

GARNISH: Orange peel, for squeezing

TOOLS

Jiggers, mixing glass, barspoon, julep strainer

GLASSWARE

Old Fashioned glass

METHOD

Add the ingredients to a mixing glass in the order indicated and stir with ice. Strain into an Old Fashioned glass over a large block of ice. Garnish with a spritz of orange oil and discard the peel.

Powers John's Lane is one of the richest, most robust whiskeys to use as a cocktail base. It's particularly suitable for stirred drinks, especially those with other rich or bitter components like this one. Pimento (or allspice) is a very potent ingredient, so make sure you're using a very small amount to start and match it to a whiskey that has substantial proof and boldness.

FEATURED SINGLE POT STILL

Powers John's Lane single pot still Irish whiskey

James Power founded his distillery at Thomas St. Dublin in 1791, moving shortly thereafter to a larger site at John's Lane near the western gate of Dublin. This expression, Powers John's Lane Release, celebrates the origin of the Powers tradition and classic style.

CALLING CARD

complex, effervescent, aromatic

Created by Greg Buda

INGREDIENTS

2 dashes house orange bitters
(page 259)

¼ ounce earl grey tea syrup
(page 252)

¼ ounce Byrrh

½ ounce Cardamaro liqueur

1¼ ounces Yellow Spot single
pot still

Champagne, to top

GARNISH: Lemon peel, for
squeezing

TOOLS

Jiggers, mixing glass, barspoon, julep
strainer

GLASSWARE

Champagne flute

METHOD

Add the bitters, Earl Grey syrup,
Byrrh, Cardamaro, and whiskey to a
mixing glass and stir with ice. Strain
into a Champagne flute without
ice. Top with Champagne and give
a light stir. Garnish with a spritz of
lemon oil and discard the peel.

Inspired by a drink Jack created for our first
menu back in 2013, Greg updated it when
Yellow Spot was launched in 2015. His use of
this high-proof twelve-year-old single pot still
whiskey, with its ex-bourbon, sherry, and Malaga
finish, makes for a fairly decadent cocktail—
definitely one to savor slowly.

FEATURED SINGLE POT STILL

Yellow Spot single pot still Irish whiskey

MEAN FIDDLER

semisweet, aromatic, full-bodied

Created by Jillian Vose

INGREDIENTS

1 dash aromatic bitters

½ teaspoon cinnamon bark syrup
(page 248)

½ ounce Campari

½ ounce green Chartreuse

¾ ounce Cocchi Storico Vermouth
di Torino

½ ounce Bowmore 12 peated single
malt Scotch

1 ounce Green Spot single pot still

GARNISH: Orange peel, for
squeezing

TOOLS

Jiggers, mixing glass, barspoon, julep
strainer

GLASSWARE

Nick & Nora glass

METHOD

Add the ingredients to a mixing glass
in the order indicated and stir with
ice. Strain into a Nick & Nora glass
without ice. Garnish with a spritz of
orange oil and discard the peel.

This is one of Jack's favorites—a take on a
Tipperary (page 82) but upgraded with accents of
cinnamon, aromatic bitters, chocolaty vermouth,
and peat. I changed out the bases to keep the
classic template intact by using Irish whiskey, but
wanted a touch of peat for complexity from the
peated Scotch. This medium-style pot still stands
up to the bold flavors of the modifiers while
giving a beautiful creaminess to the drink with
this delicate pot still Irish whiskey that also gives
a pop of bright fruit.

FEATURED SINGLE POT STILL

Green Spot single pot still Irish whiskey

DOPPELGÄNGER

earthy, herbaceous, rich

Created by Jillian Vose

INGREDIENTS

1 dash celery bitters

¼ ounce yellow Chartreuse

¾ ounce Dolin Blanc vermouth

½ ounce Linie aquavit

1½ ounces Drumshanbo single pot still

GARNISH: Lemon peel, for squeezing

TOOLS

Jiggers, mixing glass, barspoon, julep strainer

GLASSWARE

Nick & Nora glass

METHOD

Add the ingredients to a mixing glass in the order indicated and stir with ice. Strain into a Nick & Nora glass without ice. Garnish with a spritz of lemon oil and discard the peel.

This began with a challenge to create a drink geared toward a martini drinker. I chose this heavy pot still because of its higher proof, which plays well in stirred drinks and can stand up to the other strong flavors. I split the base with the aquavit, the caraway notes of which blend well with the spice of the whiskey. The yellow Chartreuse provides texture and sweetness, while the celery bitters add a distinctive savory, earthy tone.

FEATURED SINGLE POT STILL

Drumshanbo single pot still Irish whiskey

Every drop of Drumshanbo single pot still Irish whiskey has been triple-distilled at the Shed Distillery Drumshanbo using malted and unmalted Irish barley, and Irish Barra oats. Aged in single-use Kentucky bourbon casks and oloroso sherry casks, this well-balanced single pot still Irish whiskey has been created by owner PJ Rigney and Head Distiller Brian Taft.

PSYCHO KILLER

sweet, bold, strong

Created by Jillian Vose

INGREDIENTS

¾ ounce Campari

½ ounce Giffard crème de banane

½ ounce Giffard crème de cacao

2 dashes Vieux Pontarlier absinthe

2 ounces Redbreast 12 single pot still

TOOLS

Jiggers, mixing glass, barspoon, julep strainer

GLASSWARE

Old Fashioned glass

METHOD

Add the ingredients to a mixing glass in the order indicated and stir with ice. Strain into an Old Fashioned glass over a block of ice.

This is now one of our classic drinks, an Irish whiskey variation on a Boulevardier. The banana and chocolate liqueurs are a good match for the Christmas-cake qualities of the Redbreast, while the absinthe rounds it out and adds another dimension.

FEATURED SINGLE POT STILL

Redbreast 12 single pot still Irish whiskey

Redbreast holds the honor of surviving the whiskey bonder era—a time when distilleries sold whiskey directly to bonders to mature, bottle, and label. Redbreast is a 'whiskey lover's whiskey,' gathering accolades and awards across the globe, with its warm, sherry-rich character.

DARK HORSE
low ABV, dry, cleansing

Created by Gregory Buda

INGREDIENTS

1 dash Dale DeGroff's pimento bitters

¾ ounce fresh lemon juice

¼ ounce nutmeg syrup (page 264)

½ ounce banana syrup (page 240)

1 ounce Alvear pale cream sherry

1½ ounces amontillado sherry

½ ounce Green Spot single pot still

GARNISH: Nutmeg, for grating

TOOLS

Jiggers, shaker tins, fine strainer, Hawthorne strainer, nutmeg grater

GLASSWARE

Sour glass

METHOD

Add the ingredients to a shaker tin in the order indicated and shake with ice. Double strain using both the fine and Hawthorne strainers into a sour glass without ice. Garnish with a light dusting of freshly grated nutmeg.

This cocktail, a delicate low-proof sour with amontillado sherry as the base, follows the current trend toward low-ABV cocktails. I've always loved the combination of banana and amontillado, and the Green Spot provides just enough punch and body to balance the drink, with nutmeg and allspice added for complexity.

FEATURED SINGLE POT STILL

Green Spot single pot still Irish whiskey

MAGIC SPELL

floral, savory, light

Created by Long Thai

INGREDIENTS

3 dashes Combier kümmel

¼ ounce Nardini Acqua di Cedro

¾ ounce Pasquet Marie-Framboise

1 ounce R&R rosé

½ ounce Tullamore D.E.W. Caribbean rum cask

1 ounce Green Spot single pot still

GARNISH: Lemon peel, for squeezing

TOOLS

Jiggers, mixing glass, barspoon, julep strainer

GLASSWARE

Nick & Nora glass

METHOD

Add the ingredients to a mixing glass in the order indicated and stir with ice. Strain into a Nick & Nora glass without ice. Garnish with a spritz of lemon oil and discard the peel.

I'm not a big fan of kümmel, but here the contrast it provides with the other flavors is a thing of beauty. Although the rum cask–finished Tullamore D.E.W. had the right flavors, the drink needed a bit more body, so Long split the base with Green Spot, which works perfectly and doesn't outshine the qualities of the Tully Caribbean.

FEATURED SINGLE POT STILL

Green Spot single pot still Irish whiskey

FLASH POINT

citrusy, fruity, baking spice

Created by Long Thai

INGREDIENTS

¾ ounce fresh lemon juice

¼ ounce orange sherbet (page 264)

½ ounce raspberry syrup (page 267)

¼ ounce Suze

¼ ounce framboise eau-de-vie

1½ ounces Pierre Ferrand Pineau de Charentes Rouge

½ ounce raspberry-infused Green Spot (page 268)

2 ounces Peekskill sour ale

GARNISH: Nutmeg, for grating

TOOLS

Jiggers, shaker tins, fine strainer, Hawthorne strainer, nutmeg grater

GLASSWARE

Tulip beer glass

Long is our in-house beer aficionado, and he'll create drinks around the specific flavor and aroma elements of a beer. Here he took the idea of a fruit schnapps–based shandy or radler and created a cocktail with a kick that pairs raspberry to the sour ale.

FEATURED SINGLE POT STILL

Green Spot single pot still Irish whiskey

METHOD

Add the lemon juice, sherbet, raspberry syrup, pineau, Suze, and eau-de-vie to a shaker tin in the order indicated and shake with ice. Add the ale to the tin, then double strain using both the fine and Hawthorne strainers into a tulip beer glass over an ice chunk. Garnish with a light dusting of freshly grated nutmeg.

Whiskey and rebels have a long history. Seven generations of Mitchells—the family behind Spot whiskey—have been named Robert after Robert Emmet, the great Irish rebel leader.

SOUND AS A BELL

silky, dark undertones, layered

Created by Samantha Casuga & Jillian Vose

INGREDIENTS

2 dashes Bittercube blackstrap bitters

½ teaspoon fig syrup (page 254)

1 teaspoon passion fruit syrup (page 265)

½ ounce Pommeau de Normandie

½ ounce Martini & Rossi Riserva Speciale Ambrato vermouth

½ ounce Hamilton Jamaican pot still black rum

1½ ounces corn silk tea–infused Powers Three Swallow (page 250)

GARNISH: Lemon peel, for squeezing

TOOLS

Jiggers, mixing glass, barspoon, julep strainer

GLASSWARE

Small rocks glass

METHOD

Add the ingredients to a mixing glass in the order indicated and stir with ice. Strain into a small rocks glass without ice. Garnish with a spritz of lemon oil and discard the peel.

The first iteration of this drink was as a sour-style cocktail. I really liked the corn silk tea's effect on the whiskey, making it velvety and round. To not lose the texture of the infused whiskey, I kept the initial flavor pairings but made it a Sazerac serve, which is better when not ice cold.

FEATURED SINGLE POT STILL

Powers Three Swallow single pot still Irish whiskey

Powers Three Swallow Release is the 21st-century embodiment of the traditional pure pot still whiskey style that made Powers famous around the world. The name Three Swallow is deeply ingrained in Powers' history. The migration of the Irish Swallow signifies the beginning of the distillation season in Ireland, and Powers has historically used three swallows to signify the age, quality, and purity of their pot still products.

PREACHER MAN

succulent, amber, strong

Created by Jesse Vida

INGREDIENTS

2 dashes Vieux Pontarlier absinthe

¼ ounce Paolucci Amaro CioCiaro

¼ ounce Giffard crème de cacao

½ ounce Noilly Prat dry vermouth

½ ounce Carpano Antica Formula vermouth

¾ ounce Siembra Azúl reposado tequila

1 ounce Powers John's Lane single pot still

GARNISH: Orange peel, for squeezing

TOOLS

Jiggers, mixing glass, barspoon, julep strainer

GLASSWARE

Nick & Nora glass

METHOD

Add the ingredients to a mixing glass in the order indicated and stir with ice. Strain into a Nick & Nora glass without ice. Garnish with a spritz of orange oil and discard the peel.

Here Jesse took the template for a Rosita, perfect Manhattan, Greenpoint, or Carroll Gardens and plugged in a classic pot still Irish whiskey. The results are a balance of rich and dry, bold and subtle, and vanilla tamed by absinthe and amaro.

FEATURED SINGLE POT STILL

Powers John's Lane single pot still Irish whiskey

SMOOTH TALKER

dark berries, grain, sharp

Created by Long Thai

INGREDIENTS

1 dash The Bitter Truth aromatic bitters

¾ ounce fresh lemon juice

¼ ounce peach juice

¼ ounce spiced syrup (page 273)

½ ounce blackberry syrup (page 241)

½ ounce Westland sherry wood American single malt whiskey

½ ounce Irish red ale

1½ ounce Kilbeggan single pot still rye

GARNISH: Nutmeg, for grating

TOOLS

Jiggers, shaker tins, fine strainer, Hawthorne strainer, nutmeg grater

GLASSWARE

Sour glass

METHOD

Add the ingredients to a shaker tin in the order indicated and shake with ice. Double strain using both the fine and Hawthorne strainers into a sour glass without ice. Garnish with a light dusting of freshly grated nutmeg.

Another beer cocktail by Long, but this time the beer is strictly a flavor enhancer. The other flavors and the whiskey choice all stem from the flavors of the beer. The Kilbeggan rye Irish whiskey is the only whiskey on the market currently with 30 percent rye in its mash bill, which also included malted and unmalted barley (kind of like a pot still, but kind of not). This leads to a spicy, full-bodied whiskey to accompany the modifiers of blackberry, baking spice, and beer. This drink has a hearty grain component and a level of complexity and texture that is unlike any other drink in the book due to the combination of beer and whiskey chosen.

FEATURED SINGLE POT STILL

Kilbeggan single pot still rye Irish whiskey

Kilbeggan Small Batch rye is a product of the town's perseverance, as it hearkens back to the 1890s when many large Irish distillers used rye in their mash. However, the grain had virtually disappeared from the Irish whiskey category around the time of Prohibition. Double distilled in Kilbeggan's copper pot stills—one of which is the oldest working whiskey pot still in the world—it is the first of its kind and awarded Best Irish Rye in the 2020 World Whisky Awards.

SNAP DECISION

silky, bright, herbal

Created by Greg Buda

INGREDIENTS

1 dash house orange bitters
(page 259)

1 dash house cardamon bitters
(page 258)

½ teaspoon Combier L'original

1 teaspoon yellow Chartreuse

¼ ounce dried apricot syrup
(page 251)

¼ ounce Cocchi Americano

2 ounces butternut squash seed
oil–washed Powers Three Swallow
(page 243)

GARNISH: Lemon peel, for
squeezing

TOOLS

Jiggers, mixing glass, barspoon, julep
strainer

GLASSWARE

Old Fashioned glass

METHOD

Add the ingredients to a mixing glass
in the order indicated and stir with
ice. Strain into an Old Fashioned
glass over a large ice block. Garnish
with a spritz of lemon oil and
discard the peel.

Greg had discovered butternut squash seed oil
as a kitchen ingredient and decided to use it as
a fat wash in a drink. He selected Powers Three
Swallow, as it had an interesting complexity but
also a velvety softness that would let the other
flavors shine. The rest of the ingredients—apricot,
orange, herbs, and baking spice—were chosen to
complement the butternut squash.

FEATURED SINGLE POT STILL

Powers Three Swallow Irish whiskey

COMMANDER & CHIEF

stone fruit, acid, Christmas cake

Created by Jillian Vose

INGREDIENTS

2 dashes Angostura bitters

½ teaspoon passion fruit syrup (page 265)

½ teaspoon Giffard apricot

½ ounce verjus blanc

½ ounce Pommeau de Normandie

1½ ounces Redbreast Lustau single pot still

GARNISH: Lemon peel, for squeezing

TOOLS

Jiggers, mixing glass, barspoon, julep strainer

GLASSWARE

Nick & Nora glass

METHOD

Add the ingredients to a mixing glass in the order indicated and stir with ice. Strain into a Nick & Nora glass without ice. Garnish with a spritz of lemon oil and discard the peel.

Redbreast Lustau is full of fruit, tannin, and nut flavors, with a vibrant acidity to it. To create this drink, I took a Manhattan format, subbing vermouth for a Mistelle, and using Pommeau de Normandie and verjus, which bring a fantastic bright fruit element to the drink. The pommeau gives a complex baked apple note to complement the heavy sherry notes of the whiskey.

FEATURED SINGLE POT STILL

Redbreast Lustau Edition single pot still Irish whiskey

Redbreast Lustau Edition was born of a unique collaboration between Midleton and premier sherry producer Bodegas Lustau. The idea for Redbreast Lustau came from this collaboration and a desire to further marry the flavors of Redbreast and oloroso sherry. Together they collaborated on the cask selection for Redbreast's 12- and 15-year-old vintages.

LEADING LIGHT

menthol, vibrant, indulgent

Created by Ian Alexander

INGREDIENTS

½ teaspoon Vittone Fernet Menta

¼ ounce shiso syrup (page 271)

¼ ounce chinato

¼ ounce Cocchi Storico Vermouth di Torino

1 ounce white chocolate–infused Pierre Ferrand 1840 Cognac (page 278)

1 ounce raspberry-infused Green Spot (page 268)

GARNISH: Shiso tincture (page 271)

TOOLS

Jiggers, mixing glass, barspoon, julep strainer

GLASSWARE

Old Fashioned glass

METHOD

Add the ingredients to a mixing glass in the order indicated and stir with ice. Strain into an Old Fashioned glass over a block of ice. Garnish with two quick aromatized sprays of shiso tincture.

Ian once had a white-chocolate-covered shiso leaf at a restaurant, and decided to try to use that combination of flavors in a drink. He added a further raspberry element and created this Old Fashioned–style cocktail that's rich but bright.

FEATURED SINGLE POT STILL

Green Spot single pot still Irish whiskey

LOOKING GLASS

dry, briny, strong

Created by Greg Buda

INGREDIENTS

¼ ounce Avèze gentiane liqueur

¼ ounce Giffard abricot du Roussillon liqueur

½ ounce Dolin Blanc vermouth

¾ ounce Manzanilla sherry

1 ounce Don Amado Rústico mezcal

½ ounce Green Spot single pot still

GARNISH: Grapefruit peel, for squeezing

TOOLS

Jiggers, mixing glass, barspoon, julep strainer

GLASSWARE

Nick & Nora glass

METHOD

Add the ingredients to a mixing glass in the order indicated and stir with ice. Strain into a Nick & Nora glass without ice. Garnish with a spritz of grapefruit oil and discard the peel.

The fruit, floral, and light smoke of the Don Amado mezcal and Green Spot's fruit and oak qualities create a special base for this elegant stirred cocktail. I'd put this style of drink in the same category as other martini-style aged-spirit drinks like the Doppelgänger (page 131), 11th Hour (page 174), Snap Decision (page 144), Perfect Storm (page 109), Gold Digger (page 189), etc.

FEATURED SINGLE POT STILL

Green Spot single pot still Irish whiskey

WILDCAT

tropical, rich, refreshing

Created by Jesse Vida

INGREDIENTS

6 dashes cilantro tincture (page 247)

¾ ounce fresh lime juice

¾ ounce mango nectar

¼ ounce orgeat (page 265)

½ ounce Giffard crème de banane

½ ounce Giffard crème de cacao

1 ounce Jameson Black Barrel
blended Irish whiskey

1 ounce Redbreast 12 single pot still

GARNISH: Guajillo chile chocolate,
for grating

TOOLS

Jiggers, shaker tins, fine strainer,
Hawthorne strainer, nutmeg grater

GLASSWARE

Collins glass

METHOD

Add the ingredients to a shaker tin
in the order indicated and shake
with ice. Double strain using both
the fine and Hawthorne strainers
into a collins glass over cracked ice.
Garnish with a little grated chile
chocolate.

Jesse set out to make a refreshing tropical
drink with spice and texture. He wanted to use
mango juice, which is thick and masking, so he
needed a base spirit that would drive through
that. The Black Barrel is rich with vanilla, toasted
wood, and a touch of smoke, and the Redbreast
is spicy and rich. The other unusual ingredient is
the cilantro, which brings a bright vividness
to the drink.

FEATURED SINGLE POT STILL

Redbreast 12-Year-Old single pot still Irish whiskey

POWER SUPPLY

autumn, baking spices, punchy

Created by Greg Buda

INGREDIENTS

1 egg white

3 dashes Dale DeGroff Pimento bitters

3 dashes mace tincture (page 261)

1 barspoon apple butter

¼ ounce demerara syrup (page 251)

½ ounce cinnamon bark syrup (page 248)

1 ounce cask ale

1 ounce Laird's bonded applejack

1 ounce Powers John's Lane single pot still

¾ ounce half-and-half

GARNISH: Nutmeg, for grating

TOOLS

Jiggers, shaker tins, fine strainer, Hawthorne strainer, nutmeg grater

GLASSWARE

Tulip beer glass

METHOD

Add the ingredients (including the egg white) to a shaker tin and shake with ice. Double strain using both the fine and Hawthorne strainers into a tulip beer glass over a large ice chunk. Garnish with freshly grated nutmeg.

Here Greg was going for an Irish whiskey and apple flip that had some spice to it. The beer brings the sweetness level down and adds a grain component to the drink. The high-proof single pot still and bonded apple brandy are perfect for the spirit bases, and the baking spices bring it all together.

FEATURED SINGLE POT STILL

Powers John's Lane single pot still Irish whiskey

BLENDED IRISH WHISKEY COCKTAILS

SHOCK ABSORBER

playful, layered, effervescent

Created by Jillian Vose

INGREDIENTS

1 ounce Moët & Chandon Champagne

1 dash Bittered Sling Clingstone peach bitters

¾ ounce fresh lemon juice

½ ounce cantaloupe juice

¼ ounce orange sherbet (page 264)

¼ ounce vanilla syrup (page 277)

¼ ounce passion fruit syrup (page 265)

½ ounce Meletti amaro

½ ounce Mancino vermouth secco

1 ounce Roe & Co

TOOLS

Shaker tins, jiggers, fine strainer, Hawthorne strainer

GLASSWARE

Champagne flute

This idea started with the combination of cantaloupe juice, passion fruit, and peach bitters. For a base spirit, Roe & Co offers light, bright fruit and citrus notes, and a great canvas for all the complexities of the drink, melding together all of the subtle layers of the drink, as a great blended Irish whiskey should do. Think of this as a "Porn Star Martini meets Mimosa on Irish whiskey steroids"—great for brunch. Or, frankly, anytime.

FEATURED BLEND

Roe & Co Irish whiskey

METHOD

Pour the Champagne into a flute. Add the bitters, lemon juice, cantaloupe juice, orange sherbet, vanilla syrup, passion fruit syrup, amaro, vermouth, and whiskey to a shaker tin and shake with ice. Double strain using both the fine and Hawthorne strainers into the Champagne flute, filling it almost to the rim of the glass.

> While Bourbon is often synonymous with the classic mixed drinks, Roe & Co's unique use of excellent maize and barley really allows it to shine in a number of different serves, from Old Fashioneds, to Irish coffees, and the humble Highball. The inherent sweetness of the whiskey is the perfect foundation to celebrate both classic drinks and modern creations in any bar or home.

EYE CANDY

sweet, fruity, sharp

Created by Alan McGillivray

INGREDIENTS

2 dashes chamomile tincture
(page 245)

1 dash black cardamom tincture
(page 242)

¾ ounce fresh lemon juice

½ ounce fig syrup (page 254)

½ ounce cinnamon bark syrup
(page 248)

½ ounce Merlet crème de pêche

½ ounce Domaine Tariquet,
VS Bas-Armagnac (NV)

1½ ounces The Busker 'Triple Cask
Triple Smooth'

GARNISH: Nutmeg, for grating

TOOLS

Jiggers, shaker tins, fine strainer,
Hawthorne strainer, nutmeg grater

GLASSWARE

Punch glass

The Busker is great for drinks with lighter, subtler flavor pairings. I love the combination here of the fig and peach contrasted by the cardamom note, which pairs amazingly well with the ex-Cabernet wine barrel-aged whiskey.

FEATURED BLEND

The Busker 'Triple Cask Triple Smooth' Irish whiskey

METHOD

Add the ingredients to a shaker tin in the order indicated and shake with ice. Double strain into a punch glass using both the fine and Hawthorne strainers and serve with an ice nugget. Garnish with freshly grated nutmeg.

The Busker Triple Cask is a blend of high-quality single grain and a high percentage of single malt and single pot still. It is finished in bourbon, marsala, and sherry casks.

GLITTERBALL

vanilla, light, complex

Created by Jillian Vose

INGREDIENTS

1 dash mace tincture (page 261)

1 dash The Bitter Truth aromatic bitters

1 teaspoon tonka bean syrup (page 276)

½ ounce Cocchi Americano

½ ounce Domaine Tariquet VS Classique Bas-Armagnac

¾ ounce Elijah Craig bourbon

½ ounce Alvear pale cream sherry

1½ ounce Slane

GARNISH: Lemon peel, for squeezing

TOOLS

Jiggers, mixing glass, barspoon, julep strainer

GLASSWARE

Nick & Nora glass

METHOD

Add the ingredients to a mixing glass in the order indicated and stir with ice. Strain into a Nick & Nora glass without ice. Garnish with a spritz of lemon oil and discard the peel.

The components here contribute decadence and spice, nuttiness and citrus, while the Slane blended lends a distinct earthy note and some smokiness, giving it a certain mysterious quality you can't quite figure out, so you just keep sipping . . .

FEATURED BLEND

Slane Irish whiskey

As it's part of Brown Forman, Slane Irish whiskey makes two out of its three casks in-house at its own cooperages: Virgin and Seasoned. The third, Sherry, comes from a family-owned cooperage in Jerez, Spain.

BLACK ROSE

tea, aromatic, Old Fashioned

Created by Jillian Vose

INGREDIENTS

1 dash aromatic bitters

½ teaspoon Nux Alpina walnut liqueur

1 teaspoon cane syrup (page 243)

1 teaspoon Amaro Averna

½ ounce Pierre Ferrand dry curaçao

2 ounces Earl Grey tea–infused Tullamore D.E.W. 12 (page 253)

TOOLS

Jiggers, mixing glass, barspoon, julep strainer

GLASSWARE

Old Fashioned glass

METHOD

Add the ingredients to a mixing glass in the order indicated and stir with ice. Strain into an Old Fashioned glass over a large block of ice. Garnish with a spritz of orange oil and discard the peel.

Teas work best in cocktails as infusions into spirits rather than as tinctures or syrups (because they oxidize quickly). Here the Earl Grey provides warm tannin, spice, and bergamot citrus notes in a medium-bodied whiskey, which I then pair with amaro and walnut liqueur in this classic Old Fashioned variation.

FEATURED BLEND

Tullamore D.E.W. 12-Year-Old Irish whiskey

Tullamore is one of the most illustrious names in the history of Irish distilling. Production began the town of the same name in county Offaly, shifted to Dublin, then Cork, and finally back to the original site in 2014. It is a fully grain-to-glass facility, and the site also includes Tulllamore's four huge warehouses (each holding around 50,000 casks).

STRAWBERRY JAM

berries, smoke, refreshing

Created by Jack McGarry

INGREDIENTS

3 dashes Angostura bitters

¾ ounce fresh lemon juice

1 ounce strawberry syrup (page 274)

3 dashes Vieux Pontarlier absinthe

¾ ounce Braulio amaro

¾ ounce Connemara peated single malt Irish whiskey

1½ ounces hibiscus-infused Jameson Black Barrel (page 257)

1 ounce dry rhubarb soda

GARNISH: Nutmeg, for grating

TOOLS

Jiggers, shaker tins, fine strainer, Hawthorne strainer, ice pick, nutmeg grater

GLASSWARE

Mustache cup

Jameson Black Barrel is a great canvas for infusions because of its heavy pot still component, and that extra char on the barrel allows the whiskey to remain distinct in the infusion. The fruit is balanced out with absinthe, amaro, and Connemara peated Irish whiskey. The end result is a complex but very refreshing drink.

FEATURED BLEND

Jameson Black Barrel Irish whiskey

METHOD

Add the bitters, lemon juice, strawberry syrup, absinthe, amaro, Connemara, and Jameson to a shaker tin and shake with ice. Add the rhubarb soda. Double strain using both the fine and Hawthorne strainers into a mustache cup and serve with an ice nugget. Garnish with a little freshly grated nutmeg.

JOYRIDE

toasty, bright, fruity

Created by Mario Firmani and Jillian Vose

INGREDIENTS

1 dash black cardamom tincture
(page 242)

1 dash Vieux Pontarlier absinthe

¾ ounce fresh lemon juice

¼ ounce fig syrup (page 254)

½ ounce spiced pear syrup
(page 273)

¼ ounce Lustau Don Nuño oloroso
sherry

¼ ounce Dolin Génépy le Chamois

¼ ounce L'Orgeat almond liqueur

1½ ounces Dubliner blended

TOOLS

Jiggers, shaker tins, fine strainer,
Hawthorne strainer, ice pick

GLASSWARE

Coupette

METHOD

Add the ingredients to a shaker tin
in the order indicated and shake
with ice. Double strain using both
the fine and Hawthorne strainers
into a coupette and serve with an
ice nugget.

This perfect fall sour was designed around the whiskey's orchard fruit notes and richness. The fig leaf is herbaceous and vibrant, and the spiced pear brings depth against the nuttiness of the absinthe. The génépy, almond, and sherry offer complexity, while the cardamom cuts through the sweetness.

FEATURED BLEND

Dubliner blended Irish whiskey

The Dublin Liberties Distillery building dates to the 1700s and is a testament to the industry of the area—it was originally a mill, and then a tannery that specialized in rabbit skins. It is in many ways reminiscent of the heyday of masterful Dublin whiskey-making, which is again becoming renowned the world over. The distillery crafts 100 percent malted barley to be laid down for their whiskey brands, the award-winning Dubliner and Dublin Liberties whiskeys.

DEAD RINGER

rounded, spicy, tangy

Created by Jillian Vose

INGREDIENTS

1 dash turmeric citrus (page 277)

1 dash chipotle tincture (page 246)

1 teaspoon sumac syrup (page 274)

¼ ounce yellow Chartreuse

½ ounce Plantation Stiggins' Fancy pineapple rum

¾ ounce Cocchi Americano

1½ ounces Dunville's 1808 blended

GARNISH: Lemon peel, for squeezing

TOOLS

Jiggers, teaspoon, mixing glass, barspoon, julep strainer

GLASSWARE

Old Fashioned glass

METHOD

Add the ingredients to a mixing glass in the order indicated and stir with ice. Strain into an Old Fashioned glass over a large ice block. Garnish with a spritz of lemon oil and discard the peel.

Dunville's 1808 is a modern blend of malt, grain, and pot still whiskeys, strong, vivacious, and full of character. Not only do you get orchard fruits from this whiskey, but tropical notes can be pulled out as well, especially when you add pineapple rum to the mix. To offset the sweeter flavors, I've added three savory components: turmeric citrus (bright, umami), chipotle (hot spice), and sumac (tangy, spice).

FEATURED BLEND

Dunville's 1808 blended Irish whiskey

The barley for Echlinville whiskey is grown in the fields around this beautiful and historic estate in county Down. It is malted on site and distilled here in the state-of-the-art still-house: a true grain-to-glass operation. In addition to the Echlinville expressions, the distillery is reviving a lost classic of Irish whiskey, the Dunville range.

BIRTHDAY SUIT

blond, boozy, floral

Created by Jillian Vose

INGREDIENTS

2 lemon peels

2 dashes house cardamom bitters
(page 258)

2 dashes chamomile tincture
(page 245)

1 teaspoon cane syrup (page 243)

¾ ounce Cocchi Americano

Vieux Pontarlier absinthe,
for atomizer

1½ ounces Tullamore D.E.W. 12

TOOLS

Jiggers, mixing glass, atomizer

GLASSWARE

Small Old Fashioned glass

METHOD

Add the bitters, chamomile tincture, cane syrup, and Cocchi to a mixing glass. Express the oils from the lemon peels into the glass, drop in the peels, and stir with ice. Atomize 4 sprays of absinthe around and in the glass. Double strain using both the fine and Hawthorne strainers into a small Old Fashioned glass without ice.

This is a drink that's quite simple but which shows the value of a quality distillate. As this is supposed to be "blond" and not super bitter, I had to think of flavors that complemented a lighter style of drink but which were also defining. A mist of chamomile and lemon takes care of that, which just leaves making sure that the actual liquor is balanced in texture, dilution, and temperature.

FEATURED BLEND

Tullamore D.E.W. 12-Year-Old Irish whiskey

Tullamore D.E.W. 12-year-old Irish whiskey is triple cask–matured for depth and balance—a very fine aged whiskey derived from 12 to 15 years matured in a combination of bourbon and sherry casks.

FORTUNE TELLER

exuberant, puckering, strong

Created by Jillian Vose

INGREDIENTS

2 dashes Vieux Pontarlier absinthe

½ ounce Braulio amaro

¾ ounce house sweet vermouth (page 259)

¾ ounce Clear Creek cranberry liqueur

1½ ounces Dead Rabbit

GARNISH: Orange peel, for squeezing

TOOLS

Jiggers, mixing glass, barspoon, julep strainer

GLASSWARE

Nick & Nora glass

METHOD

Add the ingredients to a mixing glass in the order indicated and stir with ice. Strain into a Nick & Nora glass without ice. Garnish with a spritz of orange oil and discard the peel.

Featuring a tangy cranberry liqueur—a naturally dominating ingredient—this Manhattan variation was going to need a whiskey with a strong backbone. That is, something with a higher proof and a blend that has some spice. Dead Rabbit Irish whiskey immediately came to mind to house these bold flavors in a cocktail.

FEATURED BLEND

Dead Rabbit Irish whiskey

BEAUTY SPOT

tropical, creamy, indulgent

Created by Long Thai

INGREDIENTS

2 dashes Vieux Pontarlier absinthe

1 teaspoon matcha–Coco López mix
(page 262)

½ ounce pineapple juice

½ ounce pisatchio orgeat (page 267)

½ ounce Giffard crème de cacao

½ ounce Blume Marillen apricot
eau-de-vie

1 ounce McConnell's

¼ ounce half-and-half

GARNISH: Nutmeg, for grating

TOOLS

Jiggers, shaker tins, fine strainer,
Hawthorne strainer, nutmeg grater

GLASSWARE

Collins glass

METHOD

Add the ingredients to a shaker tin
in the order indicated and shake
with ice. Double strain using both
the fine and Hawthorne strainers
into a collins glass filled with pebble
ice. Top with more ice as needed.
Garnish with freshly grated nutmeg.

Each person brings a unique element to the
process of creating drinks. For Long, inspiration
often comes from either dining experiences
in New York or his travels around the world.
Here the spark was a particularly memorable
dessert. Think green tea and sponge cake (yes,
really), and you're in the right ballpark. This
blend of malt and grain 5-year Irish whiskey
was a perfect fit, as it adds a sweet vanilla
component while also cutting through the
richness of the drink.

FEATURED BLEND

McConnell's Irish whiskey

Established in 1776, McConnell's was once
hugely popular in Ireland and as an export.
It closed its doors in the 1930s but has
recently been revived and once again is
producing its delicate, yet robust whiskey
in the city of Belfast. This fine blend of Irish
malt and Irish grain whiskey is aged for
five years in select bourbon casks, which
bring out undertones of vanilla sweetness
with superb classic Irish whiskey quality
coming through in the background.

11TH HOUR

orchard fruit, pungent, light

Created by Jack McGarry

INGREDIENTS

3 dashes Vieux Pontarlier absinthe

½ ounce Pür Likör Williams pear liqueur

¾ ounce Cocchi Americano

¼ ounce St. George pear brandy

3 dashes Bittermens Boston Bittahs

1½ ounces Pearse Lyons 5-Year-Old

GARNISH: Lemon peel, for squeezing

TOOLS

Jiggers, mixing glass, barspoon, julep strainer

GLASSWARE

Nick & Nora glass

METHOD

Add the ingredients to your mixing glass in the order indicated and stir with ice. Strain into a Nick & Nora glass without ice. Garnish with a spritz of lemon oil and discard the peel.

This drink was meant to showcase the green grape, orchard fruit, cacao, and the strong backbone of this interesting blended whiskey. It was the first of many to showcase the light-Manhattan cocktails in our repertoire and remains popular today.

FEATURED BLEND

Pearse Lyons 5-Year-Old Irish whiskey

Pearse Lyons Distillery at St. James is a family-owned and operated distillery in the heart of the Liberties, Dublin; producing small batch malt and pot still whiskey. Mark Lyons is the seventh generation of his family involved in the Dublin whiskey industry. From start to finish every step in Pearse whiskey production is given careful attention; from growing its own grain on family land to aging its whiskey in barrels from its own sister distillery, Town Branch in Lexington Kentucky.

SUNNY-SIDE UP

Manhattan, sultry, familiar

Created by Jillian Vose

INGREDIENTS

1 dash Bittermens Xocolatl Mole bitters

1 dash Angostura bitters

¼ ounce Giffard crème de banane

¼ ounce Pierre Ferrand dry curaçao

1 ounce Cocchi Storico Vermouth di Torino

1½ ounces Tullamore D.E.W. Caribbean rum cask

TOOLS

Mixing glass, barspoon, jiggers, julep strainer

GLASSWARE

Nick & Nora glass

METHOD

Add the ingredients to a mixing glass in the order indicated and stir with ice. Strain into a Nick & Nora glass without ice.

The Caribbean rum cask finish lends the Tullamore some beautiful tropical notes, which I enhanced with the banana liqueur. This Manhattan variation is straightforward enough to be a popular drink because it reads really well and the complexity of the whiskey itself does all the talking.

FEATURED BLEND

Tullamore D.E.W. Caribbean rum cask Irish whiskey

MOOD SWING

fruity, tart, dark

Created by Jack McGarry

INGREDIENTS

2 dashes Dale DeGroff's pimento bitters

¾ ounce fresh lemon juice

¾ ounce fresh tangerine juice

½ ounce beet syrup (page 240)

¾ ounce Carpano Antica Formula vermouth

¾ ounce Clear Creek cranberry liqueur

1½ ounces Pearse Lyons 5-Year-Old

GARNISH: Nutmeg, for grating

TOOLS

Jiggers, shaker tins, fine strainer, Hawthorne strainer, nutmeg grater

GLASSWARE

Punch glass

METHOD

Add the ingredients to a shaker tin in the order indicated and shake. Double strain using both the fine and Hawthorne strainers into a punch glass and serve with an ice nugget. Garnish with freshly grated nutmeg.

Beet, cranberry, tangerine and pimento were the basis of this autumn-influenced cocktail. In place of bourbon, I chose a whiskey that had bourbon qualities but more complexity with hints of honey, chocolate, and toasted oak.

FEATURED BLEND

Pearse Lyons 5-Year-Old Irish whiskey

KING OF CLUBS

bright, tart, honey

Created by Jillian Vose

INGREDIENTS

2 sage leaves

1 barspoon kumquat preserves

½ ounce fresh lemon juice

¾ ounce Granny Smith apple juice
(page 255)

½ ounce house honey syrup
(page 257)

¼ ounce Strega

2 ounces Clonakilty port cask

TOOLS

Jiggers, barspoon, mixing tins, fine
strainer, Hawthorne strainer

GLASSWARE

Coupette

METHOD

Add the ingredients to a shaker tin
in the order indicated and shake
with ice. Double strain using both
the fine and Hawthorne strainers
into a coupette and serve with an ice
nugget.

Here I've taken a classic sour template and
melded it with a Breakfast Martini of sorts.
Instead of marmalade, I've used kumquat
preserves for a tart, bold citrus flavor. Sage
adds a soft herbaceous quality. The hint of anise
and saffron from the Strega brings the drink
together and really pair fluently with the honey
and preserves.

FEATURED BLEND

Clonakilty port cask Irish whiskey

Clonakilty matures its whiskey at its Atlantic
Ocean warehouse, 200 feet above sea level
on the family farm, the most southerly
distillery on the island of Ireland. (The
distillery also uses the farm's own barley.)

SHOOT FROM THE HIP
winter, fresh, bright

Created by Jillian Vose

INGREDIENTS

1 dash celery bitters

1 dash cilantro tincture (page 247)

¾ ounce fresh lemon juice

¼ ounce caramel cane syrup
(page 244)

½ ounce spiced pear syrup
(page 273)

½ ounce Amaro Nonino

1½ ounces Paddys blended

GARNISH: Nutmeg, for grating

TOOLS

Jiggers, shaker tins, fine strainer, Hawthorne strainer, ice tapper or cracking spoon, nutmeg grater

GLASSWARE

Julep glass

METHOD

Add the ingredients to a shaker tin in the order indicated and shake with ice. Double strain using both the fine and Hawthorne strainers into a julep glass over cracked ice. Garnish with a little freshly grated nutmeg.

The whiskey featured here has a bit of everything: single grain, pot still, and single malt, aged in both ex-bourbon and ex-sherry casks. And you can taste it all. The flavor profile of the cocktail has notes of caramel, citrus, vanilla, and dried fruits, plus cilantro and celery for complexity and Amaro Nonino for length.

FEATURED BLEND

Paddys Blended Irish whiskey

Paddys is a blended Irish whiskey produced today at the Midleton distillery in county Cork. Known for its exceptionally soft palate, Paddy is a triple-distilled blend of pot still, grain, and malt whiskeys, matured in oak for at least seven years.

FARO POINT

daiquiri, tropical, fresh

Created by Jillian Vose

INGREDIENTS

1 dash Angostura bitters

1 dash Bittermens Xocolatl Mole bitters

¾ ounce fresh lemon juice

½ ounce banana syrup (page 240)

¼ ounce orgeat (page 265)

½ ounce Pierre Ferrand Pineau des Charentes

1 ounce Plantation 5-Year-Old Barbados rum

1 ounce Teeling Small Batch

GARNISH: Nutmeg, for grating

TOOLS

Jiggers, shaker tins, fine strainer, Hawthorne strainer, ice pick, nutmeg grater

GLASSWARE

Coupette

METHOD

Add the ingredients to a shaker tin in the order indicated and shake with ice. Double strain using both the fine and Hawthorne strainers into a coupette and serve with an ice nugget. Garnish with freshly grated nutmeg.

When I was first introduced to this whiskey, its innovative rum finish intrigued me. Could I use it to rethink the daiquiri? I broke down the whiskey's flavor components and paired them with banana, chocolate, and almond. To mimic a daiquiri, it needed citrus and the right rum and, I realized, a layering modifier—that's where Pineau des Charentes comes in. And a star is born.

FEATURED BLEND

Teeling Small Batch Irish whiskey

Teeling whiskey is on a mission to share craft Irish whiskey with the world, starting with its signature flagship, Central American rum cask–finished Small Batch whiskey.

ROUGH DRAFT

umami, bitter, rich

Created by Harrison Ginsberg

INGREDIENTS

2 dashes Peychaud's bitters

1 teaspoon ginger syrup (page 255)

¾ ounce fresh lemon juice

¾ ounce white miso cane syrup
(page 279)

½ ounce Guinness stout

¼ ounce Barbadillo Pedro Ximénez
sherry

½ ounce Clear Creek eau-de-vie
pomme 8 year apple brandy

1 ounce Hinch 'The Original'

GARNISH: Nutmeg, for grating

TOOLS

Jiggers, shaker tins, fine strainer,
Hawthorne strainer, ice pick, nutmeg
grater

GLASSWARE

Smash glass

METHOD

Add the ingredients to a shaker tin
in the order indicated and shake
with ice. Double strain using both
the fine and Hawthorne strainers
into a smash glass and serve with
an ice nugget. Garnish with freshly
grated nutmeg.

This slightly sweet and salty cocktail really
explodes on the palate. The apple, ginger,
and miso really complement the notes of
marmalade, dried apricot, and earth of the
blended whiskey. The addition of Guinness, a
surprising ingredient, brings a great texture—
frothy, rich, salty, and pleasantly refreshing.

FEATURED BLEND

Hinch 'The Original' Irish whiskey

Established in 2016, Hinch is a grain-to-glass
distillery in county Down built to produce
traditional, triple-distilled Irish whiskeys that
are smooth, distinctively rich and bold.

KNEE-JERK REACTION

savory, baked apple, unique

Created by Jillian Vose

INGREDIENTS

2 dashes Dale DeGroff's pimento bitters

½ ounce Alvear pale cream sherry

1 ounce Laird's applejack

1 teaspoon coffee-pecan syrup (page 249)

1 teaspoon sweet potato syrup (page 275)

1 ounce Slane blended

GARNISH: Orange peel, for squeezing

TOOLS

Jiggers, mixing glass, barspoon, julep strainer

GLASSWARE

Old Fashioned glass

METHOD

Add the ingredients to a mixing glass in the order indicated and stir with ice. Strain into an Old Fashioned glass over a large block of ice. Garnish with a spritz of orange oil and discard the peel.

I created this explicitly with Thanksgiving or Christmas in mind. Slane has a lot of dried fruit notes and spice and goes very well with apple spirits. I used bonded applejack for some kick and also because I didn't want a lower-proof Calvados to bring too much fruit and elegance, as this drink was meant to be bold and boozy.

FEATURED BLEND

Slane Blended Irish whiskey

Slane grows both winter and spring barley on land around the distillery. The winter barley is for the pot still and grain whiskey and the spring is for malting barley, used in three types of Irish whiskey: malt, grain, and pot still, all of which are made in the distillery.

PRECISION PILOT
bright, bittersweet, revitalizing

Created by Jillian Vose

INGREDIENTS

2 dashes Peychaud's bitters

½ ounce Combier Liqueur de Pamplemousse Rose

¾ ounce Campari

1 ounce Lillet Rose

1 ounce Tullamore D.E.W. Original

GARNISH: Grapefruit peel, for squeezing

TOOLS

Jiggers, mixing glass, barspoon, julep strainer

GLASSWARE

Old Fashioned glass

METHOD

Add the ingredients to a mixing glass in the order indicated and stir with ice. Strain into an Old Fashioned glass over a large block of ice. Garnish with a spritz of grapefruit oil and discard the peel.

This was one of the first drinks I created for Dead Rabbit. The ingredients are easily accessible and the drink is not difficult to re-create. Grapefruit and Campari is one of those pairings that seems blindingly obvious in hindsight. How come no one thought of it sooner?

FEATURED BLEND

Tullamore D.E.W. Original whiskey

GOLD DIGGER

light, toasty, baking spice

Created by Jillian Vose

INGREDIENTS

2 dashes Dale DeGroff's Pimento bitters

1 teaspoon cinnamon bark syrup (page 248)

¼ ounce Pierre Ferrand Dry curaçao

¾ ounce Alvear pale cream sherry

¾ ounce Cocchi Americano

1½ ounces sesame-infused Teeling Small Batch (page 270)

GARNISH: Lemon peel, for squeezing

TOOLS

Jiggers, mixing glass, barspoon, julep strainer

GLASSWARE

Nick & Nora glass

METHOD

Add the ingredients to a mixing glass in the order indicated and stir with ice. Strain into a Nick & Nora glass without ice. Garnish with a spritz of lemon oil and discard the peel.

This Manhattan variation was built around the rum-aged whiskey. Sesame complements Small Batch well, and swapping out sweeter or more bitter vermouths for Cocchi Americano and pale cream sherry lengthened the drink and highlighted the whiskey.

FEATURED BLEND

Teeling Small Batch Irish whiskey

GREENHORN

ginger, savory, long

Created by Jillian Vose and Madeleine Solo Rapp

INGREDIENTS

1 dash celery bitters

1 dash Bittercube blackstrap bitters

¾ ounce fresh lime juice

¼ ounce ginger syrup (page 255)

½ ounce pistachio orgeat (page 267)

¼ ounce Cynar

½ ounce Linie aquavit

½ ounce Mt. Gay Black Barrel rum

1 ounce Bushmills Black Bush

GARNISH: Nutmeg, for grating

TOOLS

Jiggers, shaker tins, fine strainer, Hawthorne strainer, ice pick or cracking spoon, nutmeg grater

GLASSWARE

Collins glass

METHOD

Add the ingredients to shaker a tin in the order indicated and shake with ice. Double strain using both the fine and Hawthorne strainers into a collins glass over cracked ice. Garnish with freshly grated nutmeg.

Here, the classic Dark & Stormy cocktail is the template onto which we added with the dried fruit and malty notes of Bushmills, aged aquavit, and double-barrel rum in place of dark rum. Then we just kept going, with celery bitters and blackstrap bitters to mimic the blackstrap rum. At least we got the ginger and citrus in there.

FEATURED BLEND

Bushmills Black Bush Irish whiskey

This icon of Ireland is made of 80 percent single malt—something unheard of in a blend. In addition to its unique mash bill, Black Bush is predominantly matured in former oloroso sherry casks, offering one of the most uniquely complex whiskeys in all the world. With its rich fruity notes and deep intense character, it is often compared to a traditional Irish Christmas cake.

WITCH HUNT

tropical, beer, Old Fashioned

Created by Jillian Vose

INGREDIENTS

1 dash peach bitters

½ teaspoon cinnamon bark syrup
(page 248)

½ teaspoon Giffard crème de banane

1 teaspoon yellow Chartreuse

½ ounce Bell's IPA

2 ounces pineapple-infused Dead
Rabbit whiskey (page 266)

GARNISH: Lemon peel, for
squeezing

TOOLS

Jiggers, mixing glass, julep strainer

GLASSWARE

Old Fashioned glass

METHOD

Add the ingredients to a mixing glass
in the order indicated and stir with
ice. Strain into an Old Fashioned
glass over a large block of ice.
Garnish with a spritz of lemon oil
and discard the peel.

Tropical flavors—especially pineapple, banana,
and mango—go surprisingly well with Irish
whiskey. We chose to infuse Dead Rabbit Irish
whiskey because its virgin oak finish has strong
hits of vanilla, nuts, spice, and citrus, which go
well with the pineapple. (The higher ABV also
helps.) The IPA's distinctive hoppy, floral, and
grapefruit notes work as pair modifiers with the
tropical notes.

FEATURED BLEND

Dead Rabbit Irish whiskey

LONE OAK

whiskey sour, savory, refreshing

Created by Jillian Vose

INGREDIENTS

1 egg white

2 dashes Angostura bitters

2 fresh curry leaves

¾ ounce fresh lemon juice

1 ounce pistachio orgeat (page 267)

¼ ounce green Chartreuse

2 ounces Roe & Co

TOOLS

Jiggers, shaker tins, fine strainer, Hawthorne strainer

GLASSWARE

Coupette

METHOD

Add the ingredients to a shaker tin in the order indicated and shake with ice. Double strain using both the fine and Hawthorne strainers into a coupette over an ice nugget. Garnish with freshly grated nutmeg.

Roe & Co is an excellent whiskey for whiskey sours variations due to its higher ABV, bourbon qualities, and orchard fruit tones. Making this one with the pistachio orgeat and curry leaves was tasty, but the drink still needed something to bring it all together. A little green Chartreuse delivered; its distinctive herbal qualities providing the perfect complement.

FEATURED BLEND

Roe & Co Irish whiskey

Nestled in the heart of the infamous Liberties, Dublin, Roe & Co's Distillery pays homage to the past successes of George Roe and his family while looking to the future through constant innovation in whiskey to ensure creativity and collaboration. It will always have a home in the center of Irish whiskey production.

KINDRED SPIRIT

piña colada, tropical, complex

Created by Jillian Vose

INGREDIENTS

1 teaspoon Coco López coconut cream

½ ounce pineapple juice

¼ ounce fig syrup (page 254)

¼ ounce caramel cane syrup (page 244)

¼ ounce Grand Brulot coffee liqueur

½ ounce Montreuil Selection Calvados du Pays d'Auge

1½ ounces Tullamore D.E.W. Caribbean rum cask

¼ ounce half-and-half

GARNISH: Nutmeg, for grating

TOOLS

Jiggers, shaker tins, fine strainer, Hawthorne strainer, nutmeg grater, straw

GLASSWARE

Tulip beer glass

This was a fun take on a piña colada—fitting, since this whiskey is finished in rum barrels. The tropical notes are strong, but the contrast with the coffee liqueur really defines the drink in a way. Who'd have thought Irish whiskey could bring something to tiki!

FEATURED BLEND

Tullamore D.E.W. Caribbean rum cask Irish whiskey

METHOD

Add the ingredients to a shaker tin in the order indicated and do a short shake with 3 ice cubes. Double strain using both the fine and Hawthorne strainers into a tulip beer glass over pebble ice or crushed ice. Garnish lightly with freshly grated nutmeg. Serve with a straw.

Tullamore D.E.W. XO Caribbean rum cask finish pays tribute to the role of Irish immigrants in the development of rum in the Caribbean in the 17th century. Barrels that were previously used to age Demerara rum are carefully selected to impart distinctive tropical fruit flavors.

PAY PER VIEW

mulled spice, sangria, complex

Created by Jillian Vose

INGREDIENTS

1 dash Bittermens Xocolatl mole bitters

2 dashes Bittermens Burlesque Bitters

¼ ounce fresh lemon juice

¼ ounce rhubarb syrup (page 268)

½ ounce raspberry syrup (page 267)

2 ounce mulled dubonnet (page 263)

1½ ounces Slane

GARNISH: Nutmeg, for grating

TOOLS

Jiggers, shaker tins, nutmeg grater

GLASSWARE

Fancy wineglass

METHOD

Add the ingredients to a shaker tin in the order indicated and whip shake with 10 pieces of pebble ice. Pour into a fancy wineglass over cracked ice without straining. Garnish with freshly grated nutmeg.

I'd recently opened a bottle of Dubonnet Rouge to mix a rare drink from an old menu for a guest, and the next day decided to use the bottle to make a seasonal mulled wine. I treated it like sangria and added fruit syrups. It still needed body and a bit of boozy bite, so I reached for Slane, a perfect medium-bodied blended whiskey with a heavy wood influence.

FEATURED BLEND

Slane Irish whiskey

The distillery is a stone's throw from Slane Castle, home to the Conyngham family since 1703, and is built in the castle's former stables and farm buildings. There are no horses there anymore but you'll find a sculpture of one made from barrel staves and hoops in the distillery garden.

IRISH COFFEE MARTINI

pick-me-up, frothy, coffee

Created by Jillian Vose

INGREDIENTS

1 dash Bitter Truth aromatic bitters

½ ounces demerara syrup
(page 251)

1½ ounces drip coffee (page 252)

1½ ounces Bushmills Black Bush

GARNISH: Lemon peel, for
squeezing

TOOLS

Jiggers, shaker tins, fine strainer,
Hawthorne strainer

GLASSWARE

Nick & Nora glass

METHOD

Add the ingredients to a shaker tin
in the order indicated and shake
with ice. Double strain using both
the fine and Hawthorne strainers
into a Nick & Nora glass over
cracked ice. Garnish with a spritz of
lemon oil and discard the peel.

We often get asked for Espresso Martinis at the
bar but could never properly execute them,
as we don't keep an espresso machine. As a
solution, we went with cold brew, as it's not as
acidic as espresso and is also appealing to Irish
coffee drinkers looking for a cool, refreshing
caffeine hit in a cocktail.

FEATURED BLEND

Bushmills Black Bush Irish whiskey

TIME TRAVELER

apple, approachable, long

Created by Erin Smyth

INGREDIENTS

3 dashes Vieux Pontarlier absinthe

¾ ounce fresh lemon juice

1 ounce Granny Smith apple juice
(page 255)

¾ ounce fennel syrup (page 254)

½ ounce fino sherry

½ ounce Avèze gentiane liqueur

1½ ounces Tullamore D.E.W. 12

TOOLS

Jiggers, shaker tins, fine strainer,
Hawthorne strainer

GLASSWARE

Taproom highball glass

METHOD

Add the ingredients to a shaker tin
in the order indicated and shake
with ice. Double strain using both
the fine and Hawthorne strainers
into a taproom highball glass over
cracked ice.

The green apple note that comes through in
this whiskey was Erin's initial inspiration for
the drink. She then layered in absinthe, apple
juice, and lemon, making a great, approachable
cocktail, especially for people just getting into
loving Irish whiskey.

FEATURED BLEND

Tullamore D.E.W. 12-Year-Old Irish whiskey

MOONWALK

tantalizing, complex, bright

Created by Samantha Casuga

INGREDIENTS

1 dash walnut Angostura bitters
(page 278)

1 dash Bittermens winter melon bitters

½ teaspoon St. George pear eau-de-vie

1 teaspoon Giffard crème de cacao

¼ ounce spiced syrup (page 273)

¼ ounce Lustau Manzanilla Papirusa
sherry

¼ ounce St-Germain elderflower
liqueur

1 ounce Connemara peated single malt

1 ounce Tullamore D.E.W. 12

GARNISH: Lemon peel, for squeezing

TOOLS

Jiggers, mixing glass, julep strainer

GLASSWARE

Old Fashioned glass

METHOD

Add the ingredients to a mixing glass
in the order indicated and stir with ice.
Strain into an Old Fashioned glass over
a block of ice. Garnish with a spritz of
lemon oil and discard the peel.

There are a lot of ingredients here, and no, it's
not the easiest drink to make at home. But it's
worth giving a try for the wonderful clusters
of flavor pairings: spice, orchard fruit, flower,
peat, vanilla. Tullamore D.E.W. 12 makes for a
silky backdrop and ensures the peatiness of the
Connemara just lingers subtly in the background
without taking over.

FEATURED BLEND

Tullamore D.E.W. 12-Year-Old Irish whiskey

SCARLET LADY

raspberry, spice, effervescent

Created by Jillian Vose

INGREDIENTS

1 dash Bittermens 'Elemakule Tiki bitters

¼ ounce cane syrup (page 243)

½ ounce Pasquet Marie-Framboise

¼ ounce Amaro Montenegro

1 ounce Bushmills Black Bush

Champagne, to top

GARNISH: Nutmeg, for grating

TOOLS

Jiggers, mixing glass, ice pick, nutmeg grater

GLASSWARE

Julep glass

METHOD

Add the bitters, cane syrup, Marie-Framboise, amaro, and whiskey to a mixing glass and lightly stir. Pour into a julep glass over cracked ice and top with Champagne. Garnish with freshly grated nutmeg.

The idea here was to pair raspberry and spice into a Champagne cobbler template with a fitting Irish whiskey. I opted for Marie-Framboise, which is Pineau des Charentes steeped with raspberries, while Amaro Montenegro brings multiple baking spice notes as well as orange and vanilla.

FEATURED BLEND

Bushmills Black Bush Irish whiskey

BROKEN PROMISE

coconut, coffee, long

Created by Aidan Bowie, Mario Firmani, and Jillian Vose

INGREDIENTS

1 dash cherry bark vanilla bitters

1 teaspoon Grand Brulot coffee liqueur

¼ ounce fresh lemon juice

½ ounce spiced guinness syrup (page 272)

¼ ounce Brennivín Rúgbraud aquavit

1 ounce coconut-infused el dorado white rum (page 248)

1 dash Vieux Pontarlier absinthe

1 ounce Slane

2 ounces soda water

GARNISH: Lemon peel, for squeezing

TOOLS

Jiggers, shaker tin

GLASSWARE

Highball glass

We'd been thinking about a whiskey-based coffee-and-tonic-style cooler. We started with the coffee liqueur Grand Brulot and house coconut rum for depth and tropical notes, but then: which whiskey? Slane's multi-cask influences on a grain/malt blend were perfect. The drink was still a bit sweet, so we added a touch of fresh lemon. Finally, the cherry bark vanilla bitters bounced off the whiskey like fireworks.

FEATURED BLEND

Slane Irish whiskey

METHOD

Add the bitters, Brulot, lemon juice, guinness syrup, aquavit, rum, absinthe, and whiskey to a shaker tin and whip shake with 10 pieces of pebble ice until the ice is completely melted. Add 2 ounces of soda to the tin, then pour into a highball glass over cracked ice. Garnish with a spritz of lemon oil and discard the peel.

Slane Castle has hosted more than 1 million music fans at its concerts since 1981 featuring some of the best-known artists of the last four decades. It's also served as the recording studio for a chart-topping album.

FLIGHT ATTENDANT

Manhattan, familiar, bitter

Created by Nick Rolin

INGREDIENTS

1 dash Bittermens Xocolatl Mole bitters

¼ ounce Cappelletti Amaro Sfumato Rabarbaro

¼ ounce Giffard crème de cacao

¼ ounce Merlet crème de fraise des bois

¾ ounce house sweet vermouth (page 259)

1½ ounces Dublin Liberties 5-Year-Old 'Oak Devil'

GARNISH: Orange peel, for squeezing

TOOLS

Jiggers, mixing glass, barspoon, julep strainer

GLASSWARE

Nick & Nora glass

METHOD

Add the ingredients to a mixing glass in the order indicated and stir with ice. Strain into a Nick & Nora glass without ice. Garnish with a spritz of orange oil and discard the peel.

The higher proof and rough, woody notes of the whiskey cut through any sweetness of the other components in this drink. Mole bitters give a sharp chocolate note, while the crème de cacao is more milk chocolate. The amaro has a unique bitter, smoky element to it and really makes this drink stand out. Though it reads quite fruity, it's a great alternative to a classic Manhattan.

FEATURED BLEND

Dublin Liberties 5-Year-Old 'Oak Devil' Irish whiskey

The Liberties area was driven by industry, legal and not, where tanners, distillers, and merchants traded side by side, and brothels, illicit taverns, and gambling houses were loved by criminals and the cream of society alike. This area in the Liberties became known as "hell." To enter hell, you needed to walk under an archway where a carved oak devil stood.

SPEED DEMON

apple, complex, boozy

Created by Jillian Vose

1 dash Dale DeGroff's Pimento Bitters

¼ ounce dried apricot syrup (page 251)

½ ounce verjus

¼ ounce Becherovka

½ ounce Pierre Ferrand Pineau des Charentes

1½ ounces Tullamore D.E.W. cider cask

GARNISH: Lemon peel, for squeezing

TOOLS

Jiggers, mixing glass, barspoon, julep strainer

GLASSWARE

Nick & Nora glass

METHOD

Add the ingredients to a mixing glass in the order indicated and stir with ice. Strain into a Nick & Nora glass without ice. Garnish with a spritz of lemon oil and discard the peel.

When creating this drink, I was really doing an Irish whiskey version of an Apple Martini. The Becherovka brought some cinnamon and herbaceousness to the drink for depth, almost giving it a spiced-apple-pie vibe. One of my favorites.

FEATURED BLEND

Tullamore D.E.W. cider cask Irish whiskey

ANIMAL INSTINCT

bright, floral, light

Created by Shane Mulvany

INGREDIENTS

1 dash cinnamon Angostura bitters
(page 247)

2 dashes rice vinegar

1 ounce chamomile honey syrup
(page 245)

1 ounce Calvados Lelouvier

½ ounce Léonce vermouth

¾ ounce Sauternes

1 ounce West Cork Glengarriff
bog oak charred cask

GARNISH: Lemon peel, for
squeezing

TOOLS

Jiggers, mixing glass, barspoon, julep
strainer

GLASSWARE

Nick & Nora glass

METHOD

Add the ingredients to a mixing
glass in the order indicated and stir
with ice. Strain into a Nick & Nora
glass without ice. Garnish with a
spritz of lemon oil and discard the
peel.

This drink showcases just how elegantly Irish
whiskey can play in the right company. There
is quite a bit of acidity in this one, with the
Sauternes, rice vinegar, and chamomile, so the
bog oak charred cask was a great choice as a
counterpoint to the lighter ingredients.

FEATURED BLEND

West Cork Glengarriff bog oak charred cask Irish whiskey

SMART MOVE

anise, aromatic, bright

Created by Kevin Baird

INGREDIENTS

1 egg white

2 dashes rose water

1 ounce fresh lime juice

½ ounce celery juice

¾ ounce macadamia orgeat
(page 260)

¼ ounce Giffard crème de cacao

½ ounce absinthe

1½ ounces Roe & Co

GARNISH: Lemon peel, for
squeezing

TOOLS

Jiggers, shaker tins, fine strainer,
Hawthorne strainer

GLASSWARE

Sour glass

METHOD

Add the ingredients to a shaker tin
in the order indicated. Dry shake
without ice, then shake with ice.
Double strain using both the fine
and Hawthorne strainers into a sour
glass without ice. Garnish with a
spritz of lemon oil and discard the
peel.

Kevin had never seen an Irish whiskey–based
Suissesse cocktail before (well, nobody had),
so he set out to create one. Roe & Co is a great
canvas for other flavors and also brings a lot
of vanilla to the front, which pairs nicely with
the macadamia orgeat. Celery juice kind of puts
a whole new twist to the drink. Absinthe and
celery also make a great duo.

FEATURED BLEND

Roe & Co Irish whiskey

Roe & Co's Signature blended whiskey
delivers on the promise of the nose to
instantly gratify guests, customers, or friends.
A task not so easily undertaken by Master
Blender Caroline Martin, there are few
people who tend to turn their nose up to
the luscious, ripe orchard fruit, decadent
caramel, and creamy vanilla that follows
throughout the whole tasting experience.

SPELL SPOKE

bright, aromatic, refreshing

Created by Jillian Vose

INGREDIENTS

2 dashes Bittermens Boston Bittahs

4 dashes lime leaf tincture
(page 260) or 2 fresh lime leaves

¾ ounce fresh lime juice

¾ ounce cane sugar

¼ ounce ginger syrup (page 255)

2 ounces hibiscus-infused Jameson
Black Barrel (page 257)

GARNISH: Nutmeg, for grating

TOOLS

Jiggers, shaker tins, fine strainer,
Hawthorne strainer, nutmeg grater

GLASSWARE

Highball glass

METHOD

Add the ingredients to a shaker tin
in the order indicated and shake
with ice. Double strain using both
the fine and Hawthorne strainers
into a highball glass over cracked
ice. Garnish with freshly grated
nutmeg.

This is a take on a daiquiri I created using
hibiscus-infused whiskey, lime, and cane syrup,
accented with a hint of ginger. It still needed
something, though, so I dashed in the bright
chamomile and citrus bitters and added some
vibrant fresh lime leaves to the tin, which really
make the drink pop.

FEATURED BLEND

Jameson Black Barrel Irish whiskey

OLD TIMER

light Manhattan, herbal, complex

Created by Shane Mulvany

1 dash The Bitter Truth aromatic bitters

1 dash Vieux Pontarlier absinthe

1 teaspoon Italicus bergamot liqueur

¼ ounce Meletti amaro

¼ ounce Punt e Mes vermouth

¾ ounce Martini & Rossi Bianco vermouth

2 ounces Dead Rabbit

GARNISH: Orange peel, for squeezing

TOOLS

Jiggers, mixing glass, barspoon, julep strainer

GLASSWARE

Nick & Nora glass

METHOD

Add the ingredients to a mixing glass and stir with ice. Strain into a Nick & Nora glass without ice. Garnish with a squeeze of orange oil and discard the peel.

This Manhattan variation is a nod to the boozy version New York is known for, but with a lighter twist, using more Bianco vermouth than the bitter Punt e Mes. While there is a hint of Meletti amaro to insinuate that there's more bitterness, this particular amaro is on the softer side and is quite cinnamon-forward.

FEATURED BLEND

Dead Rabbit Irish whiskey

WANDERLUST

flip, orchard fruit, decadent

Created by Jesse Vida

INGREDIENTS

1 egg

1 dash aromatic bitters

½ ounce orgeat (see page 265)

¼ ounce Giffard crème de cacao

½ ounce pear eau-de-vie

½ ounce Merlet crème de poire Williams

1½ ounces Hinch 5-Year-Old double wood

½ ounce heavy cream

GARNISH: Nutmeg, for grating

TOOLS

Jiggers, shaker tins, fine strainer, Hawthorne strainer, nutmeg grater

GLASSWARE

Tulip beer glass

METHOD

Add the ingredients to a shaker tin in the order indicated and shake with ice. Double strain using both the fine and Hawthorne strainers into a tulip beer glass over a chunk of ice. Garnish with freshly grated nutmeg.

For most cocktail bars, these ingredients are pretty common, making this flip very accessible. Hinch 5 year was a great choice for this because of the ex-bourbon and Virgin American oak finish, lending spice, vanillin, fruit, and smoke to the mix. The layered pear flavors and toasted almond syrup go seamlessly with the custard and chocolate of the whiskey as well.

FEATURED BLEND

Hinch 5-Year-Old double wood Irish whiskey

VICEROY

nostalgic, nutty, long

Created by Jillian Vose

INGREDIENTS

2 drops sarsaparilla tincture
(page 269)

2 dashes saline solution (page 269)

2 dashes Angostura bitters

¾ ounce lemon juice

1 ounce vanilla syrup (page 277)

½ ounce Williams & Humbert Dry
Sack medium sherry

¾ ounce Siembre Azul Reposado
tequila

1 ounce Slane

1 ounce soda water, to top

GARNISH: Nutmeg, for grating

TOOLS

Jiggers, shaker tins, fine strainer,
Hawthorne strainer, barspoon,
nutmeg grater

GLASSWARE

Collins glass

I'd never really worked with sarsaparilla before, and decided to create a cocktail that tasted like an adult cream soda. Vanilla and the beautifully rich Siembra Azul and the trio-cask finished Slane did the trick. This drink reminds me a great summer day on Cape Cod.

FEATURED BLEND

Slane Irish whiskey

METHOD

Add the bitters, sarsaparilla tincture, lemon juice, vanilla syrup, saline solution, tequila, sherry, and whiskey to a shaker tin in the order indicated and give a short shake with 3 ice cubes. Double strain using both the fine and Hawthorne strainers into a collins glass over cracked ice. Add the soda, give a light stir, and serve. Garnish with grated nutmeg.

BOX OFFICE

fruit, smoke, rich

Created by Ian Alexander, Melissa Markert, and Long Thai

INGREDIENTS

1 dash Angostura bitters

1 dash chipotle tincture (page 246)

1 teaspoon strawberry syrup
(page 274)

1 teaspoon John D. Taylor Velvet
Falernum

½ ounce verjus

½ ounce Pineau des Charentes

½ ounce Bowmore 12 peated single
malt Scotch

1½ ounces mango-infused Teeling
Small Batch (page 261)

GARNISH: Lemon peel, for
squeezing

TOOLS

Jiggers, mixing glass, barspoon, julep
strainer

GLASSWARE

Old Fashioned glass

METHOD

Add the ingredients to a mixing
glass in the order indicated and
stir with ice. Strain into an Old
Fashioned glass over a large block
of ice. Garnish with a spritz of
lemon oil and discard the peel.

Here you get fruitiness from the strawberry
and mango infusion, and the juiciness is
maintained by the acid of the verjus and pineau,
all brought together by this tropical medium-
bodied Irish whiskey. The surprise is the
chipotle, which makes you go back for another
sip, and another . . .

FEATURED BLEND

Teeling Small Batch Irish whiskey

DOUBLE WHAMMY

mai tai, dessert, spic

Created by Kevin Baird

INGREDIENTS

1 dash The Bitter Truth aromatic
bitters

2 dashes mace tincture (page 261)

¾ ounce fresh lime juice

½ ounce marshmallow syrup
(page 262)

½ ounce pistachio orgeat (page 267)

½ ounce Combier L'Original
triple sec

1 ounce Mount Gay Eclipse rum

1 ounce West Cork bourbon cask

GARNISH: Nutmeg, for grating

TOOLS

Jiggers, shaker tins, fine strainer,
Hawthorne strainer, nutmeg grater

GLASSWARE

Old Fashioned glass

METHOD

Add the ingredients to a shaker tin
and whip shake with 3 ice cubes.
Double strain using both the fine
and Hawthorne strainers into an
Old Fashioned glass over pebble
ice or crushed ice. Garnish with a
dusting of freshly grated nutmeg.

Kevin set out to make an Irish whiskey mai tai,
and started by keeping one half of the base rum
and then some of the sweeteners as an orange
liqueur (Combier). The other sweeteners pair
things that matched both Irish whiskey and
rum. The West Cork ex-bourbon whiskey has a
unique rustic vibe, and its vanilla notes pair well
with the marshmallow and pistachio.

FEATURED BLEND

West Cork bourbon cask Irish whiskey

QUALITY CONTROL

Manhattan, herbal, peat

Created by Jillian Vose

INGREDIENTS

1 dash The Bitter Truth aromatic bitters

1 teaspoon Varnelli Amaro Sibilla

¼ ounce Caffo Amaretto

½ ounce sapin

¾ ounce Cocchi Storico Vermouth di Torino

¼ ounce Bowmore 12 peated single malt Scotch

1½ ounces Dead Rabbit

GARNISH: Orange peel, for squeezing

TOOLS

Jiggers, mixing glass, barspoon, julep strainer

GLASSWARE

Nick & Nora glass

METHOD

Add the ingredients to a mixing glass in the order indicated and stir with ice. Strain into a Nick & Nora glass without ice. Garnish with a spritz of orange oil and discard the peel.

The contrast of peated Scotch and Irish whiskey is an amazing thing: the two work astonishingly well together. Amaretto complements the maturation of the whiskey, sapin (pine liqueur) gives herbal notes and texture, and the Sibilla is an immensely bitter and complex amaro where a little goes a long way.

FEATURED BLEND

Dead Rabbit Irish whiskey

PRAYING MANTIS
warming, aromatic, orange

Created by Jillian Vose

INGREDIENTS

2 dashes Angostura bitters

½ teaspoon acid phosphate

¾ ounce mulled Pedro Ximénez sherry (page 263)

2 ounces Bushmills Black Bush

Hot water, to top

GARNISH: Nutmeg, for grating

TOOLS

Jiggers, nutmeg grater

GLASSWARE

Hot toddy glass

METHOD

Add the bitters, acid phosphate, sherry, and whiskey to a warm toddy glass. Top with hot water and give a light stir. Garnish with freshly grated nutmeg.

Every winter we love to have something to offer for a hot drink in addition to our beloved Irish coffee option. The Black Bush yields some great dried fruit notes that work amazingly well in this reimagined mulled wine–type drink. You can find acid phosphate to purchase at artofdrink.com.

FEATURED BLEND

Bushmills Black Bush Irish whiskey

The Bushmills Distillery, the oldest licensed in the world, was created in 1608 when King James I granted a distilling license to Sir Thomas Phillips. Overcoming wars, fires, and famine, Bushmills has remained true to its Irish roots and carries forward a style of whiskey that is both the standard for Ireland and a direct link to the very origins of whiskey. As they like to say of the distillery, "They're not the best because they're the oldest, they're the oldest because they're the best."

JUMPING JACK

apple spice, rich, effervescent

Created by Long Thai

INGREDIENTS

1 dash Bittermens 'Elemakule' Tiki bitters

2 dashes Vieux Pontarlier absinthe

½ ounce fresh lemon juice

¼ ounce cane syrup (page 243)

½ ounce cinnamon bark syrup (page 248)

½ ounce Pierre Ferrand Pineau des Charentes

1 ounce Laird's applejack

1 ounce Jameson Black Barrel

Dry vanilla soda, to top

GARNISH: Nutmeg, for grating

TOOLS

Jiggers, shaker tins, fine strainer, Hawthorne strainer, nutmeg grater

GLASSWARE

Mustache cup

Long's idea was to play off the baking spice of the applejack and the bourbon-noted Jameson Black Barrel and accentuate them with the bitters and sweeteners. To not oversweeten the drink, he added Pineau des Charentes for some acidity and used a dry soda instead of something that would contribute more sugar. The result is a perfect early autumn cocktail.

FEATURED BLEND

Jameson Black Barrel Irish whiskey

METHOD

Add the bitters, lemon juice, cane syrup, cinnamon syrup, pineau, absinthe, applejack, and whiskey to a shaker tin and shake with ice. Double strain using both the fine and Hawthorne strainers into a mustache cup over an ice nugget. Top with vanilla soda and garnish with freshly grated nutmeg.

CULTURE SHOCK

citrus, tea, peat

Created by Long Thai

INGREDIENTS

4 dashes earl grey tincture
(page 253)

¾ ounce fresh lemon juice

½ ounce fennel syrup (page 254)

1 ounce grilled pineapple–infused
Bols genever (page 256)

½ ounce Giffard crème de cacao

1 ounce Connemara peated single
malt

1 ounce Roe & Co

GARNISH: Nutmeg, for grating

TOOLS

Shaker tins, jiggers, fine strainer,
Hawthorne strainer, nutmeg grater

GLASSWARE

Coupette

METHOD

Add the ingredients to a shaker tin
in the order indicated and shake
with ice. Double strain using both
the fine and Hawthorne strainers
into a coupette and serve with an ice
nugget. Garish with freshly grated
nutmeg.

Roe & Co is mostly a grain base, which gives the cocktail a lighter, refreshing mouthfeel. Genever boosts the body and brings a savory hint. Pineapple gives the cocktail enough juiciness to stand up to the fennel and cacao. The Earl Grey (a black tea with bergamot oil) boosts the cocoa element, while the Connemara's smoky aroma brings everything to the next level.

FEATURED BLEND

Roe & Co Irish whiskey

From its repurposed home of the old Guinness Power Station in the heart of Dublin, Roe & Co Distillery Company uses prideful errors of Irish whiskey past to inform their humble experimentation with different mash builds, maturation, and yeast strains. This direction ensures a bright future for both the current smallest whiskey distillery in Diageo's portfolio and the category itself.

BITE THE BULLET
Manhattan, tropical, layered

Created by Jillian Vose

INGREDIENTS

1 dash The Bitter Truth aromatic bitters

½ teaspoon vanilla syrup (page 277)

1 teaspoon Giffard Caribbean pineapple liqueur

¼ ounce Becherovka

1 ounce Cocchi Storico Vermouth di Torino

1½ ounces Glendalough Double Barrel

TOOLS

Jigger, mixing glass, julep strainer

GLASSWARE

Nick & Nora glass

METHOD

Add the ingredients to a mixing glass in the order indicated and stir with ice. Strain into a Nick & Nora glass without ice and serve.

This is a Manhattan variation with tropical notes that play well with the vanilla, chocolate, and toasted oak flavors of the Glendalough Double Barrel whiskey. You'll get pineapple, cinnamon, vanilla, and chocolate flavors out of this drink, though not in a sweet way. Becherovka brings an herbal quality, along with cinnamon and ginger, plus a certain dryness due to the higher proof of the liqueur.

FEATURED BLEND

Glendalough Double Barrel Irish whiskey

Glendalough relentlessly searches for the finest, most flavorful species of oak to age and finish their Irish whiskeys—from the wooded mountains surrounding Hokkaido in the very north of Japan to the forested hills and valleys of northern Spain. Their casks are crafted by true craftsmen, like master Hidetoshi Ichitsubo, who has spent his life in pursuit of perfection—a necessary trait if you are to cooper Mizunara oak successfully.

POWDER KEG

nostalgic, warming, chocolate

Created by Jillian Vose and Nick Rolin

INGREDIENTS

¼ ounce demerara syrup (page 251)

½ ounce banana syrup (page 240)

¼ ounce amontillado sherry

¼ ounce Myrus nutmeg liqueur

¼ ounce green Chartreuse

4 ounces chocolate oat milk
(page 246)

1 ounce Bushmills Black Bush

Heavy cream, to top

GARNISH: Nutmeg, for grating

TOOLS

Jiggers, plastic bottle, hot water bath,
nutmeg grater

GLASSWARE

Teacup

Nick and I had come up with a Scotch-based hot chocolate cocktail that was such a hit, we decided to morph it into a permanent menu item, but featuring Irish whiskey. Bushmills Black Bush with its sweet malty tones and dried berries was a no-brainer when it came to pairing with the banana, nutmeg, green Chartreuse, and sherry modifiers. We simply adjusted the sugar up from the original recipe (the other one was boozier) and the drink was perfect. This drink can also be dairy-free if you omit the cream top.

FEATURED BLEND

Bushmills Black Bush Irish whiskey

METHOD

Add the demerara syrup, banana syrup, chocolate oat milk, sherry, nutmeg liqueur, Chartreuse, and whiskey into a plastic bottle, and shake well. Keep in a hot water bath at 80°C (176°F). When the mixture comes up to temperature, pour into a teacup and top with cream to serve. Garnish with freshly grated nutmeg.

POWERPOINT

bright, sour, approachable

Created by Jillian Vose

INGREDIENTS

1 dash cilantro tincture (page 247)

1 ounce fresh lime juice

¼ ounce spiced pear syrup
(page 273)

½ ounce pistachio orgeat (page 267)

½ ounce Martini & Rossi Riserva
Speciale Ambrato vermouth

¼ ounce green Chartreuse

2 ounces Roe & Co

GARNISH: Nutmeg, for grating

TOOLS

Jiggers, shaker tins, fine strainer,
Hawthorne strainer, nutmeg grater

GLASSWARE

Sour glass

METHOD

Add the ingredients to a shaker
tin in the order indicated and shake
with ice. Double strain using both
the fine and Hawthorne strainers
into a sour glass without ice. Garnish
with freshly grated nutmeg.

This a sour format featuring orchard fruit
and almonds along with the whiskey. Using
vermouths in citrusy cocktails is a great
trick to add a touch of light aromatics and
herbaceousness to a drink without bitterness.
Roe & Co is a lighter style of whiskey, best used
with ingredients that won't overpower it but
will pull out the vanillin and wood tones of the
grain-heavy blend.

FEATURED BLEND

Roe & Co Irish whiskey

CHIP AND PIN

Martinez, subtle spice, tropical, unique

Created by Jillian Vose

INGREDIENTS

1 dash cherry bark vanilla bitters

2 dashes Bittermens Hellfire habanero shrub

½ teaspoon orgeat (page 265)

½ teaspoon Giffard Caribbean pineapple liqueur

1 teaspoon Xila licor de agave liqueur

¾ ounce Carpano Antica Formula sweet vermouth

1½ ounces Rutte Old Simon genever

½ ounce Tullamore D.E.W. Caribbean rum cask

TOOLS

Jiggers, mixing glass, barspoon, julep strainer

GLASSWARE

Nick & Nora glass

METHOD

Add the ingredients to a mixing glass in the order indicated and stir with ice. Strain into a Nick & Nora glass without ice.

Everything about this drink screams "rich." As for flavors, I started with a Martinez template, intending to use Irish whiskey as a split base with the gin. From there, in place of maraschino, I opted for a flavor combo of cherry bark, cooked pineapple, and chile to match the tropical Caribbean rum cask–finished whiskey and vanilla-heavy sweet vermouth.

FEATURED BLEND

Tullamore D.E.W. Caribbean rum cask Irish whiskey

THE FUTURE IS AMBER

by Jack McGarry

It's been said that history is news that stays news. In other words, the past remains relevant to the present and the future. The same can be said of Irish whiskey, which today is in its most exciting and dynamic phase in generations. The long history and enduring legacy of the great distillers serve as inspirations for a new generation, and those inspirations are taking many forms. While some of today's new distillers are learning from the masters and producing bottlings in that tradition, others are looking at more innovative approaches—some of which are designed expressly for use in cocktails and mixed drinks. And still others are doing both.

At the time of this writing, Ireland has some 28 operating Irish whiskey distilleries with another 22 in development. It's estimated that by 2025, these 50 could be producing over 20 million cases of whiskey a year, possibly even overtaking Scotch in the United States within a decade—a clear indication of the growth, demand, and energy driving the sector today.

We are seeing single grain, single malt, and single pot still Irish whiskeys expanding their market shares. Interest in premium and collectible Irish whiskeys is growing exponentially, too.

WHAT ELSE WILL WE SEE?

In short, we are entering a new age of experimentation and innovation. As distilleries in Ireland begin releasing their mature stocks, we can expect to see significant experimentation with different mash bills, distillation styles, and wood maturation programs. IDL presciently recognized this and built a microdistillery at Midleton in 2015 solely for innovation. Another forward-thinker within the industry is the Teeling whiskey Company, where master distiller Alex Chasko dedicates 25 percent of the distillery's output to experimentation and is currently incorporating nontraditional malts, aquavit cask-finishing, and proprietary yeast strains into his whiskeys.

We can also expect to hear the term "terroir" more frequently, exemplified by the work of Mark Reynier. His Waterford Distillery works with over seventy farmers. Each farm is located in a different region, with a unique soil type and microclimate, and each may use a different strain of barley or a particular agricultural approach, such as organic or biodynamic.

Waterford sources grain from more than forty of these farmers in any given year. Each farmer provides the distillery with grain, which is then used to brew and distill unique batches of whiskey. This comparative approach allows for an unprecedented analysis of the contribution of raw material (the barley) to finished product (the whiskey).

MARKETS OLD AND NEW

The Americas constitute Irish whiskey's primary market, accounting for more than 50 percent of global sales. Emerging markets include Ireland (yes, more of us are drinking our own native spirit), duty-free outlets, Russia, and Central Europe. Consumption in Africa and Asia is in its infancy, with plenty of room to grow.

The Americas are projected to record sales of 8 to 10 million cases of Irish whiskey by 2024; Europe, Australia, and duty-free will account for 5 to 6 million cases; and Russia and Eastern Europe will sell 2 to 3 million cases. Africa and Asia are projected to consume 1 to 2 million cases each, bringing total sales of Irish whiskey somewhere between 16 and 21 million cases worldwide.

IN CONCLUSION

With the number of distilleries in Ireland rapidly increasing, and consumer interest growing to match, we are at the beginning of an exciting time for the category. We're seeing innovative new labels and expressions coming to the market, a rise in Irish whiskey tourism, and of course ever-greater use of Irish whiskey in cocktails.

And there's much, much more to come. The future looks good—and it is cast in exquisite shades of richest, deepest amber.

SYRUPS, TINCTURES, AND INFUSIONS

The recipes in this chapter yield 750 ml (25 fluid ounces) to more than 1 L (34 fluid ounces). If you'd like to make smaller batches for home use, we suggest dividing the ingredient quantities by 4.

BANANA SYRUP

YIELD

1 L (34 fluid ounces)

INGREDIENTS

1 L (34 fluid ounces) cane syrup (page 243)

170 g (6 ounces) peeled bananas, frozen

TOOLS

Vacuum bag, vacuum sealer, immersion circulator, water bath

METHOD

Combine the syrup and bananas in a vacuum bag. Vacuum-seal the bag and sous-vide in a water bath at 45°C (113°F) for 12 hours. Strain through a fine-mesh strainer. Bottle, label, and store in the refrigerator. Keeps for up to 10 days.

BEET SYRUP

YIELD

1.25 L (42 fluid ounces)

INGREDIENTS

9 to 10 whole beets

250 ml (8.5 fluid ounces) water

750 g (26 ounces) sugar

TOOLS

Juice extractor, induction cooktop

METHOD

Juice the beets using a juice extractor; you'll need 500 ml (17 fluid ounces) of beet juice. Strain the beet juice through a colander or fine-mesh strainer into a medium size stainless-steel pot. Add the water and sugar and heat at 70°C (158°F), whisking frequently, until the sugar has completely dissolved, about 5 minutes. Pour into a container and let cool for 10 minutes. Bottle, label, and store in the refrigerator. Keeps for up to 1 week.

BLACKBERRY SHRUB

YIELD

750 ml (25 fluid ounces)

INGREDIENTS

200 g (7 ounces/2 pints) blackberries

500 g (17.5 ounces) sugar

Zest of 1 lime

500 ml (17 fluid ounces) apple cider vinegar

TOOLS

Citrus zester, vacuum bag, vacuum sealer, induction cooktop, cheesecloth

METHOD

Combine the blackberries, sugar, and lime zest in a vacuum bag. Vacuum-seal the bag, mash the contents together, and refrigerate overnight. The next day, pour the contents of the bag into a medium size stainless-steel pot and add the vinegar. Heat at 80°C (176°F), whisking frequently, until the sugar has completely dissolved. Strain through cheesecloth. Bottle, label, and store in the refrigerator. Keeps for up to 2 weeks.

BLACKBERRY SYRUP

YIELD

1 L (34 fluid ounces)

INGREDIENTS

1 L (34 fluid ounces) semi-rich simple syrup (page 270)

200 g (7 ounces) blackberries

7 ml (¼ fluid ounce) Everclear or high-proof vodka

TOOLS

¼-ounce jigger, vacuum bag, vacuum sealer, immersion circulator, water bath, cheesecloth

METHOD

Combine the syrup, blackberries, and Everclear in a vacuum bag. Vacuum-seal and sous-vide in a water bath at 52°C (125.6°F) for 4 hours. Strain the contents of the bag through cheesecloth. Bottle, label, and store in the refrigerator. Keeps for up to 2 weeks.

BLACK CARDAMOM TINCTURE

YIELD

1 L (34 fluid ounces)

INGREDIENTS

28 g (1 ounce) black cardamom, crushed

500 ml (17 fluid ounces) Everclear or high-proof vodka

500 ml (17 fluid ounces) water

TOOLS

Spice grinder

METHOD

Lightly grind or pulse the cardamom using a spice grinder. Combine the Everclear and cardamom in an airtight container and let sit at room temperature for 72 hours. Strain through a fine-mesh strainer and mix in the water. Bottle, label, and store at room temperature. Keeps for up to 3 months.

BLACK PEPPER TINCTURE

YIELD

1 L (34 fluid ounces)

INGREDIENTS

3 tablespoons ground black peppercorns

500 ml (17 ounces) Everclear or other high-proof neutral spirit

500 ml (17 ounces) water

TOOLS

Non-reactive airtight container to hold 1 L (34 fluid ounces), cheesecloth or coffee filter

METHOD

Mix the pepper and Everclear in an airtight container and let sit at room temperature for 72 hours. Strain through cheesecloth or a coffee filter and mix in the water. Bottle, label, and store at room temperature. Keeps for up to 3 months.

BUTTERNUT SQUASH SEED OIL–WASHED POWERS THREE SWALLOW

YIELD

1 L (34 fluid ounces)

INGREDIENTS

1 L (34 fluid ounces) Powers Three Swallow Irish whiskey

60 ml (2 fluid ounces) butternut squash seed oil

TOOLS

2-ounce jigger, non-reactive airtight container to hold 1 L (34 fluid ounces), coffee filter

METHOD

Combine the whiskey and oil in an airtight container. Let sit at room temperature for 4 hours. Place in the freezer for 24 to 48 hours, until the oil has frozen. Strain through a fine-mesh strainer lined with a coffee filter. Bottle, label, and store at room temperature. Keeps for up to 3 months.

CANE SYRUP

YIELD

1 L (34 fluid ounces)

INGREDIENTS

500 ml (17 fluid ounces) water

1 kg (35 ounces) evaporated cane juice

TOOLS

Induction cooktop

METHOD

Combine the sugar and water in a medium size stainless-steel pot and heat over medium heat, stirring until the sugar has completely dissolved. Bring the syrup to a rolling boil, then remove from the heat and let cool. Bottle, label, and store in the refrigerator. Keeps for up to 4 weeks.

CARAMEL CANE SYRUP

YIELD

1.5 L (50 fluid ounces)

INGREDIENTS

500 ml (17 fluid ounces) caramel sauce

1 L (34 fluid ounces) cane syrup (page 243)

TOOLS

Hot water bath, blender

METHOD

Place the caramel sauce in a hot water bath until it is pourable. Pour the caramel sauce and cane syrup into a blender and blend for 1 minute. Bottle, label, and store in the refrigerator. Keeps for up to 2 months.

CARROT-INFUSED PLANTATION 3 STARS WHITE RUM

YIELD

750 ml (25 fluid ounces)

INGREDIENTS

200 g (7 ounces) sliced peeled carrots

750 ml (25 fluid ounces) Plantation 3 Stars white rum

TOOLS

Vegetable peeler, vacuum bag, vacuum sealer, immersion circulator, water bath, cheesecloth

METHOD

Place the carrots in a vacuum bag and pour in the rum. Vacuum-seal the bag and sous-vide in a water bath at 70°C (158°F) for 4 hours. Strain the contents of the bag through cheesecloth. Bottle, label, and store in the refrigerator. Keeps for up to 3 months.

CHAMOMILE HONEY SYRUP

YIELD

890 ml (30 fluid ounces)

INGREDIENTS

1 chamomile tea bag (2.5 g/0.09 ounce)

300 ml (10 fluid ounces) hot water

565 g (20 ounces) clover honey

TOOLS

Large bowl or other vessel, hot water bath

METHOD

Place the chamomile tea bag in a large bowl or other vessel, pour in the hot water, and steep for 7 minutes. Meanwhile, soften the honey by placing the jar in a hot water bath. Discard the tea bag. Whisk the honey together with 1.2 L (40 ounces) of the warm chamomile tea. Bottle, label, and store in the refrigerator. Keeps for up to 2 weeks.

CHAMOMILE TINCTURE

YIELD

1 L (34 fluid ounces)

INGREDIENTS

500 ml (17 fluid ounces) Everclear or high-proof vodka

56 g (2 ounces) dried chamomile flowers

500 ml (17 fluid ounces) water

METHOD

Combine the Everclear and chamomile in an airtight container and let sit at room temperature for 72 hours. Strain through a fine-mesh strainer and whisk in the water. Bottle, label, and store at room temperature. Keeps for up to 3 months.

CHIPOTLE TINCTURE

YIELD

1 L (34 fluid ounces)

INGREDIENTS

57 g (2 ounces) dried chipotle chiles

500 ml (17 fluid ounces) Everclear or high-proof vodka

500 ml (17 fluid ounces) water

TOOLS

Plastic gloves

METHOD

Wearing gloves, shred the chiles, exposing their seeds. Combine the chiles and the Everclear in an airtight container and let sit at room temperature for 72 hours. Strain through a fine-mesh strainer and whisk in the water. Bottle, label, and store at room temperature. Keeps for up to 3 months.

CHOCOLATE OAT MILK

YIELD

1.25 L (42 fluid ounces)

INGREDIENTS

1 L (34 fluid ounces) oat milk

2 tablespoons unsweetened dark cocoa powder

2 tablespoons sugar

¼ teaspoon agar-agar

TOOLS

Blender

METHOD

Place the oat milk, cocoa powder, sugar, and agar-agar in a blender and blend until completely combined. Bottle, label, and store in the refrigerator. Keeps for up to 1 week (check the expiration date of the oat milk to confirm).

CILANTRO TINCTURE

YIELD

945 ml (32 fluid ounces)

INGREDIENTS

57 g (2 ounces) fresh cilantro

500 ml (17 fluid ounces) Everclear

500 ml (17 fluid ounces) water

METHOD

Combine the cilantro and Everclear in an airtight container and let sit at room temperature for 72 hours. Strain through a fine-mesh strainer and add the water. Bottle, label, and store at room temperature. Keeps for up to 3 months.

CINNAMON ANGOSTURA BITTERS

YIELD

300 mL (about 10 fluid ounces)

INGREDIENTS

300 mL (10 fluid ounces) Angostura bitters

50 g (1¾ ounces) Vietnamese cassia cinnamon bark

TOOLS

Spice grinder, non-reactive container, coffee filter

METHOD

Break cinnamon bark into small pieces, then place in a saucepan over low heat to toast—do not burn. Remove from heat to cool. Coarsely grind bark in a spice grinder. In a non-reactive container, combine bitters and cassia and let macerate for 4 hours. Strain through a coffee filter. Bottle, label, and store at room temperature. Keeps for up to 3 months.

CINNAMON BARK SYRUP

YIELD

750 ml (25 fluid ounces)

INGREDIENTS

20 g (0.7 ounces) cassia cinnamon bark

500 ml (17 fluid ounces) water

500 g (17.5 ounces) superfine sugar

TOOLS

2 large zipper-top plastic bags, muddler, induction cooktop

METHOD

Place the cinnamon bark in one of the plastic bags. On a safe and hard surface, use the muddler to crush the bark. (Even better: Buy it crushed.) Transfer the crushed bark to a medium size stainless-steel pot and add the water and sugar. Bring to a boil, whisking frequently, then remove from the heat. Transfer to an airtight container and let sit at room temperature for 12 hours. Strain through a fine-mesh strainer. Bottle, label, and store in the refrigerator. Keeps for up to 2 weeks.

COCONUT-INFUSED EL DORADO WHITE RUM

YIELD

1 L (34 fluid ounces)

INGREDIENTS

100 g (3.5 ounces) unsweetened coconut flakes, toasted

1 L (34 fluid ounces) El Dorado 3-Year-Old Demerara white rum

TOOLS

Sauté pan, vacuum bag, vacuum sealer, immersion circulator, water bath, coffee filter

METHOD

Toast the coconut flakes in a medium sauté pan over medium heat until golden brown and fragrant. Transfer the toasted coconut to a vacuum bag and pour in the rum. Vacuum-seal and sous-vide in a water bath at 52°C (125.6°F) for 8 hours. Refrigerate overnight. Strain the contents of the bag through a coffee filter. Bottle, label, and store in the refrigerator. Keeps for up to 3 months.

COFFEE-PECAN SYRUP

YIELD

5 L (170 fluid ounces)

INGREDIENTS

1 kg (35 ounces) pecans

2.4 kg (84 ounces) fine sugar

500 ml (17 fluid ounces) black drip coffee (page 252)

1 kg (35 ounces) cane sugar

2 tablespoons ground chicory root

30 ml (1 fluid ounce) Everclear

TOOLS

Induction cooktop, food processor, cheesecloth

METHOD

Place pecans in a medium stainless-steel pot and cover with water. Simmer at 60°C (140°F) for 30 minutes. Strain and blend the pecans in a food processor until smooth. Add 2.4 L (10 cups) hot water to the blended pecans and let soak for 2 hours. Strain through cheesecloth and place into the pot with the fine sugar. Cook at 70°C (158°F), stirring occasionally until completely dissolved. Add the coffee, cane sugar, and chicory. Stir to dissolve the sugar. Turn off the heat and let sit, covered, for 1 hour. Strain through cheesecloth. Add the Everclear. Bottle, label, and store in the refrigerator. Keeps for up to 2 weeks.

CORIANDER-INFUSED GLENMORANGIE 10

YIELD

1 L (34 fluid ounces)

INGREDIENTS

2 tablespoons coriander seed, crushed

1 L (34 fluid ounces) Glenmorangie 10-Year-Old Highland single malt Scotch

TOOLS

Spice grinder, non-reactive airtight container to hold 1 L (34 fluid ounces), coffee filter or cheesecloth

METHOD

Pulse the coriander in a spice grinder and transfer to an airtight container. Add the Glenmorangie and let sit at room temperature, stirring occasionally, for 1 hour. Strain through a coffee filter or cheesecloth. Bottle, label, and store at room temperature. Keeps for up to 3 weeks.

CORN SILK TEA-INFUSED POWERS THREE SWALLOW

YIELD

750 ml (25 fluid ounces)

INGREDIENTS

2 g (0.07 ounce) loose corn silk tea or 2 corn silk tea bags

1 (750 ml/25 fluid ounces) bottle Powers Three Swallow

METHOD

Combine the corn silk tea and the whiskey in an airtight container and let sit at room temperature for 15 minutes. Strain through a fine-mesh strainer or remove and discard the tea bags. Bottle, label, and refrigerate for up to 3 months.

DEAD RABBIT JAMAICA RUM BLEND

YIELD

1.875 L (63 ounces)

INGREDIENTS

750 ml (25 fluid ounces) Smith & Cross Jamaica rum

750 ml (25 fluid ounces) Cruzan blackstrap rum

375 ml (13 fluid ounces) Banks 7 Golden Age rum

TOOLS

Large bowl

METHOD

Combine all the rums in a large bowl and mix well. Bottle, label, and store at room temperature; as long as the bottle is kept sealed during storage, this will keep for years.

DEMERARA SYRUP

YIELD

1 L (34 fluid ounces)

INGREDIENTS

1 kg (35 ounces) demerara sugar

500 ml (17 ounces) water

TOOLS

Induction cooktop

METHOD

Place the sugar and water in a medium size stainless-steel pot and mix well. Heat at 80°C (176°F), whisking, until the sugar has completely dissolved. Bring to a rolling boil, then remove from the heat and let cool. Bottle, label, and refrigerate for up to 4 weeks.

DRIED APRICOT SYRUP

YIELD

1.5 L (50 fluid ounces)

INGREDIENTS

200 g (7 ounces) dried apricots, chopped

1 L (34 fluid ounces) water

750 g (26 ounces) sugar

TOOLS

Induction cooktop, cheesecloth

METHOD

Combine the apricots and water in a medium size stainless-steel pot. Bring to a boil over medium-high heat, then reduce the heat to low and simmer until the liquid has reduced by one-quarter (about 750 ml/25 fluid ounces). Remove from the heat and let cool for 30 minutes. Strain the mixture through cheesecloth and return it to the pot. Add the sugar and heat at 70°C (158°F), stirring frequently, until the sugar has completely dissolved. Bottle, label, and store in the refrigerator. Keeps for up to 2 weeks.

DRIP COFFEE

YIELD

1.5 L (50 fluid ounces)

INGREDIENTS

1.7 L (56 fluid ounces) water

85 g (3 ounces) medium ground Sumatra
Mandheling coffee or other dark, fruity roast

TOOLS

Drip coffee maker

METHOD

Prepare the drip coffee according to your
drip coffee maker manual. Store in the
refrigerator in an airtight container. Keeps
for up to 2 days.

EARL GREY TEA SYRUP

YIELD

1 L (34 fluid ounces)

INGREDIENTS

500 ml (17 fluid ounce) Earl Grey tea (strong)
made with 85 g (3 ounces) Earl Grey loose
leaf tea leaves, or 3 Earl Grey tea bags

1 kg (35 ounces) superfine sugar

TOOLS

Induction cooktop, coffee filter (if using
loose tea)

METHOD

Combine the tea and sugar in a medium-
size stainless-steel pot and bring to a boil
over medium-high heat, stirring frequently.
Remove from the heat and let cool for 1 hour.
(Caution: Cooling the syrup too quickly or
unevenly will result in recrystallization of the
sugar.) Strain the syrup through a fine-mesh
strainer and/or coffee filter. Bottle, label,
and store in the refrigerator. Keeps for up
to 1 week.

EARL GREY TINCTURE

YIELD

1 L (34 fluid ounces)

INGREDIENTS

85g (3 ounces) (3 teabags) Earl Grey tea

500 ml (17 fluid ounces) Everclear

500 ml (17 fluid ounces) water

TOOLS

Airtight container to hold 1 L (34 fluid ounces)

METHOD

Combine the tea and Everclear in an airtight container and steep at room temperature for 72 hours. Strain through a fine-mesh strainer and add the water. Bottle, label, and store at room temperature. Keeps for up to 3 months.

EARL GREY TEA-INFUSED TULLAMORE D.E.W. 12

YIELD

750 ml (25 fluid ounces)

INGREDIENTS

1 tablespoon loose leaf Earl Grey Tea

1 (750 ml) bottle Tullamore Dew 10 Year

TOOLS

Cheesecloth

METHOD

Flash steep the tea with hot water and strain immediately to rinse away some of the tannins. Then soak the tea in the whiskey for 5 minutes. Strain with cheesecloth or coffee filter. Bottle, label and store at room temperature. Keeps for up to 3 months.

FENNEL SYRUP

YIELD

1 L (34 fluid ounces)

INGREDIENTS

28 g (1 ounce) fennel seed, crushed

750 g (26 ounces) superfine sugar

750 ml (25 fluid ounces) water

TOOLS

Spice grinder, induction cooktop, cheesecloth

METHOD

Lightly grind the fennel seed in a spice grinder and transfer to a medium size stainless-steel pot. Add the sugar and water and heat at 80°C (176°F). Bring to a boil, stirring frequently. Remove from the heat and let cool for 1 hour. Strain through cheesecloth. Bottle, label, and store in the refrigerator. Keeps for up to 2 weeks.

FIG SYRUP

YIELD

1 L (34 fluid ounces)

INGREDIENTS

170 g (6 ounces) stemmed dried Mission figs, quartered

750 ml (25 fluid ounces) water

750 g (26 ounces) superfine sugar

TOOLS

Induction cooktop

METHOD

Combine the figs and water in a medium size stainless-steel pot and heat at 80°C (176°F). Bring to a boil, then reduce the heat to 60°C (140°F) and simmer for 1 hour. Strain through a fine-mesh strainer, return the liquid to the pot, and add the sugar. Heat at 60°C (140°F), stirring frequently, until the sugar has completely dissolved. Bottle, label, and store in the refrigerator. Keeps for up to 2 weeks.

GINGER SYRUP

YIELD

1 L (34 fluid ounces)

INGREDIENTS

750 ml (25 fluid ounces) fresh ginger juice

750 g (26 ounces) superfine sugar

TOOLS

Juice extractor, induction cooktop, cheesecloth

METHOD

Strain the ginger juice through a fine-mesh strainer into a medium size stainless-steel pot. Whisk in the sugar and heat at 70°C (158°F) for 45 minutes, stirring occasionally. Remove from the heat and let cool to room temperature. Strain through cheesecloth. Bottle, label, and store in the refrigerator. Keeps for up to 2 weeks.

GRANNY SMITH APPLE JUICE (ACID ADJUSTED)

YIELD

1 L (34 fluid ounces)

INGREDIENTS

1 L (34 fluid ounces) fresh apple juice

1 teaspoon ascorbic acid

TOOLS

Juice extractor, large bowl

METHOD

Strain the apple juice through a fine-mesh strainer into a large bowl. Add the ascorbic acid and whisk thoroughly. It is important to add the acid ASAP to impede the oxidization of the juice. Bottle, label, and store in the refrigerator. Keeps for up to 3 days.

GRENADINE

YIELD

1 L (34 fluid ounces)

INGREDIENTS

500 ml (17 fluid ounces) POM Wonderful pomegranate juice

250 ml (8 fluid ounces) water

750 g (26 ounces) sugar

TOOLS

Induction cooktop

METHOD

Combine the pomegranate juice, water and sugar in a medium size stainless-steel pot and heat at 70°C (158°F), stirring occasionally, until the sugar has completely dissolved. Remove from the heat and let cool for 15 minutes. Bottle, label, and store in the refrigerator. Keeps for up to 2 weeks.

GRILLED PINEAPPLE-INFUSED BOLS GENEVER

YIELD

1 L (34 fluid ounces)

INGREDIENTS

½ ripe pineapple, sliced

1 L (34 fluid ounces) Bols Jonge Graangenever (unaged genever)

TOOLS

Grill, tongs, non-reactive airtight container to hold 1 L (34 fluid ounces)

METHOD

Heat your grill to 204°C (400°F). Grill the pineapple slices for 5 minutes on each side, or until each side has char marks. Transfer the pineapple to an airtight container, add the Bols, refrigerate overnight, then strain. Bottle, label, and store in the refrigerator. Keeps for up to 3 months.

HIBISCUS-INFUSED JAMESON BLACK BARREL

YIELD

1 L (34 fluid ounces)

INGREDIENTS

2 tablespoons dried hibiscus flowers

1 L (34 fluid ounces) Jameson Black Barrel Irish whiskey

TOOLS

Non-reactive airtight container to hold 1 L (34 fluid ounces), colander, cheesecloth or coffee filter

METHOD

Combine the hibiscus flowers and whiskey in an airtight container and let sit for 30 minutes. Strain through a colander lined with cheesecloth or a coffee filter. Bottle, label, and store at room temperature. Keeps for up to 3 months.

HOUSE HONEY SYRUP

YIELD

Yield varies

INGREDIENTS

2 parts honey syrup

1 part cane syrup (page 243)

TOOLS

Bowl

METHOD

Combine the syrups in a bowl in a 2:1 ratio. Bottle, label, and store in the refrigerator. Keeps for up to 4 weeks.

HOUSE CARDAMOM BITTERS

YIELD

175 ml (6 fluid ounces)

INGREDIENTS

150 ml (5 fluid ounces) Regans' Orange Bitters No. 6

30 ml (1 fluid ounce) Scrappy's cardamom bitters

METHOD

Combine both bitters in an airtight container, seal the lid, and give it a good shake. Transfer to a dasher bottle, label, and store at room temperature. Keeps indefinitely.

HOUSE MARASCHINO LIQUEUR

YIELD

Yield varies

INGREDIENTS

1 part Luxardo maraschino liqueur

1 part Clear Creek cherry brandy (kirschwasser)

METHOD

Pour all the ingredients into an airtight container, seal the lid, and mix well. Bottle, label, and store at room temperature. Keeps indefinitely.

HOUSE ORANGE BITTERS

YIELD

Yield varies

INGREDIENTS

1 part Regans' Orange Bitters No. 6

1 part Angostura orange bitters

METHOD

Combine equal parts of both bitters in an airtight container, seal the lid, and give it a good shake. Transfer to a dasher bottle, label, and store at room temperature. Keeps indefinitely.

HOUSE SWEET VERMOUTH

YIELD

1.5 L (50 fluid ounces)

INGREDIENTS

750 ml (25 fluid ounces) Martini & Rossi Rosso vermouth

750 ml (25 fluid ounces) Punt e Mes vermouth

TOOLS

Large bowl or other vessel (2 L or larger)

METHOD

Combine the vermouths in a large airtight container and mix well. Bottle, label, and store in the refrigerator. Keeps for up to 2 weeks.

LIME LEAF TINCTURE

YIELD

1 L (34 fluid ounces)

INGREDIENTS

10 fresh lime leaves

500 ml (17 fluid ounces) Everclear or high-proof vodka

500 ml (17 fluid ounces) water

TOOLS

Airtight container to hold 1 L (34 fluid ounces)

METHOD

Combine the Everclear and lime leaves in an airtight container and let sit at room temperature for 72 hours. Strain and mix in the water. Bottle, label, and store at room temperature. Keeps for up to 3 months.

MACADAMIA ORGEAT (AKA MACDADDY)

Orgeat is historically made from barley and almond, but now anything made from grains or nuts can be considered an orgeat—so this is our modern and clarified version of it. Make it from scratch with our version of the recipe (or purchase from orgeatworks.com, as we do).

YIELD

1 L (34 fluid ounces)

INGREDIENTS

1 cup whole macadamia nuts

1 cup superfine sugar

1 cup water

4 orange peels

TOOLS

Sterile 1 L (34 fluid ounce) container with lid, Superbag

METHOD

Crush macadamia nuts and then add nuts, sugar, and water together in a pot. Put over heat and bring to a boil while stirring until sugar is dissolved. Take off heat. Express orange peels over syrup. Cover and let sit in a refrigerated area for 24 hours. Strain with a Superbag and add 30 ml (1 fluid ounce) of Everclear or high-proof vodka. Bottle, label, and store in the refrigerator. Keeps for up to 1 week.

MACE TINCTURE

YIELD

1 L (34 fluid ounces)

INGREDIENTS

3 tablespoons crushed mace blades

500 ml (17 fluid ounces) Everclear or high-proof vodka

500 ml (17 fluid ounces) water

TOOLS

Spice grinder, airtight container, cheesecloth or coffee filter

METHOD

Pulse the mace in a spice grinder, making sure not to grind it too fine, then transfer to an airtight container. Add the Everclear and let sit at room temperature for 72 hours. Strain through cheesecloth or a coffee filter and mix with the water. Bottle, label, and store at room temperature. Keeps for up to 3 months.

MANGO-INFUSED TEELING SMALL BATCH

YIELD

1 L (34 fluid ounces)

INGREDIENTS

200 g (7 ounces) frozen mango

750 ml (25 fluid ounces) Teeling Small Batch blended Irish whiskey

TOOLS

Vacuum bag, vacuum sealer, immersion circulator, water bath, Superbag

METHOD

Place the mango in a vacuum bag and pour in the whiskey. Vacuum-seal the bag and sous-vide in a water bath at 52°C (125.6°F) for 6 hours. Strain the contents of the bag through a Superbag. Bottle, label, and store in the refrigerator. Keeps for up to 3 months.

MATCHA-COCO LÓPEZ MIX

YIELD

425 g (15 ounces)

INGREDIENTS

1 (425 g/15-ounce) can Coco López cream of coconut

1 tablespoon matcha green tea powder

TOOLS

Blender

METHOD

Combine the cream of coconut and matcha in blender and blend until smooth and evenly green in color. Pour into an airtight container, label, and store in the refrigerator. Keeps for up to 2 weeks. (When in use, hold at room temperature for ease.)

MARSHMALLOW SYRUP

YIELD

475 ml (16 fluid ounces)

INGREDIENTS

235 ml (8 fluid ounces) cane sugar

235 ml (8 fluid ounces) water

8 large marshmallows

TOOLS

Mixing vessel, large pot, induction cooktop

METHOD

Toast/char marshmallows until the outer surfaces are completely dark. Add the water and sugar slowly. Heat until marshmallows and sugar are completely dissolved, but do not let the mixture boil, to avoid thickening. Bottle, label, and store in the refrigerator. Keeps for up to 2 weeks.

MULLED DUBONNET

YIELD

750 ml (25 fluid ounces)

INGREDIENTS

1 whole nutmeg

10 whole cloves

20 allspice berries

30 g (1 ounce) cassia cinnamon bark

750 ml (25 fluid ounces) Dubonnet Rouge

TOOLS

Hammer or mallet, vacuum bag, vacuum sealer, immersion circulator, water bath, cheesecloth

METHOD

Crack the whole nutmeg with the hammer or mallet and place it in a vacuum bag. Add the cloves, allspice, and cassia bark and pour in the Dubonnet. Vacuum-seal the bag and sous-vide in a water bath at 50°C (122°F) for 3 hours. Strain the contents of the bag through cheesecloth. Bottle, label, and store in the refrigerator. Keeps for up to 2 weeks.

MULLED PEDRO XIMÉNEZ SHERRY

YIELD

1 L (34 fluid ounces)

INGREDIENTS

1 whole nutmeg

10 whole cloves

2 bay leaves

20 allspice berries

30 g (1 ounce) cassia cinnamon bark

Zest of 1 orange

425 ml (15 fluid ounces) Rhum Clément Creole Shrubb

750 ml (25 fluid ounces) Lustau Pedro Ximénez sherry

TOOLS

Citrus zester, hammer or mallet, vacuum bag, vacuum sealer, immersion circulator, water bath, cheesecloth

METHOD

Crack the nutmeg with a hammer or mallet and place it in a vacuum bag. Add the cloves, bay leaves, allspice, cassia bark, and orange zest, then pour in the Shrubb and sherry. Vacuum-seal and sous-vide in a water bath at 50°C (122°F) for 3 hours. Strain the contents of the bag through cheesecloth. Bottle, label, and store in the refrigerator. Keeps for up to 2 weeks.

NUTMEG SYRUP

YIELD

1 L (34 fluid ounces)

INGREDIENTS

1 kg (35 ounces) superfine sugar

20 g (0.7 ounce) freshly grated nutmeg

500 ml (17 fluid ounces) water

TOOLS

Nutmeg grater, induction cooktop, cheesecloth

METHOD

Combine the sugar, nutmeg, and water in a medium size stainless-steel pot and heat at 80°C (176°F), stirring occasionally, for 30 minutes, or until the sugar has completely dissolved. Remove from the heat and let cool for 1 hour. Strain through cheesecloth. Bottle, label, and store in the refrigerator. Keeps for up to 2 weeks.

ORANGE SHERBET

YIELD

1 L (34 fluid ounces)

INGREDIENTS

Zest of 4 oranges

750 g (26 ounces) fine sugar

750 ml (25 fluid ounces) orange juice

TOOLS

Zester, induction cooktop, vacuum bag (optional), vacuum sealer (optional)

METHOD

Combine the zest and sugar in a medium bowl, making sure to mix them thoroughly so that the oils from the zest begin to express into the sugar. Let sit at room temperature for 1 hour. (Alternatively, you can vacuum seal the zest and sugar together to get faster or more thorough results in less time.) Put the orange sugar into a medium size stainless-steel pot and add the orange juice. Heat at 60°C (140°F), stirring regularly, until the sugar has completely dissolved, about 30 minutes. Remove from the heat and strain through a fine-mesh strainer. Bottle, label, and store in the refrigerator. Keeps up to 1 week.

ORGEAT

YIELD

1 L (34 fluid ounces)

If you're not feeling up to making orgeat from scratch, purchase from orgeatworks.com, as we do.

INGREDIENTS

250 g (9 ounces) blanched almonds

600 g (21 ounces) superfine sugar

1 teaspoon orange flower water

7 ml (¼ ounce) Everclear or high-proof vodka

600 ml (20 fluid ounces) hot water

TOOLS

Induction cooktop, food processor, cheesecloth

METHOD

Place the almonds in a pot and add water to cover, then cover the pot. Heat at 60°C (86°F) for 30 minutes. Drain and transfer to a food processor; process until smooth. Transfer the almond paste to an airtight container, add the hot water, and let sit at room temperature for 2 hours. Strain through cheesecloth back into the pot (you should have about 450 ml/15 fluid ounces). Add the sugar (with the quantity adjusted to a 4:3 ratio to the almond milk) and orange flower water. Cook at 70°C (158°F), stirring occasionally, until the sugar has completely dissolved. Remove from the heat and mix in the Everclear. Let cool. Bottle, label, and store in the refrigerator. Keeps for up to 3 weeks.

PASSION FRUIT SYRUP

YIELD

1 L (34 fluid ounces)

INGREDIENTS

1 kg (35 ounces) superfine sugar

500 ml (17 fluid ounces) Ceres passion fruit juice

TOOLS

Induction cooktop, airtight container

METHOD

Combine the sugar and juice in a medium size stainless-steel pot and heat at 80°C (176 °F), stirring frequently, until it comes to a boil. Remove from the heat and transfer to an airtight container; let cool for 1 hour. Bottle, label, and store in the refrigerator. Keeps for up to 2 weeks.

PECAN ORGEAT

YIELD

About 1 L (34 fluid ounces)

INGREDIENTS

250 g (9 ounces) pecans, crushed

600 ml (20 fluid ounces) hot water

600 g (21 ounces) superfine sugar

7 ml (¼ fluid ounce) Everclear or high-proof vodka

TOOLS

Induction cooktop, food processor, Superbag, ¼-ounce jigger

METHOD

Place the pecans in a medium size stainless-steel pot and add water to cover. Heat at 60°C (140°F) for 30 minutes. Drain the pecans, then transfer them to a food processor and process until smooth. Transfer to an airtight container, add the hot water to the pecan paste and let sit for 2 hours. Strain the mixture back into the pot through a Superbag (you should have about 1.5 L/50 fluid ounces pecan milk) and add the sugar. Cook at 70°C (158°F), stirring occasionally, until the sugar has completely dissolved. Remove from the heat. Mix in the Everclear and let cool. Bottle, label, and store in the refrigerator. Keeps for up to 2 weeks.

PINEAPPLE-INFUSED DEAD RABBIT WHISKEY

YIELD

1 L (34 fluid ounces)

INGREDIENTS

1 L bottle Dead Rabbit whiskey

200g frozen pineapple chunks

TOOLS

Vacuum bag, vacuum sealer, cheesecloth

METHOD

Place pineapple in a vacuum bag and pour in the whiskey. Seal the bag and sous-vide at 45°C for 6 hours. Strain contents through a cheesecloth. Bottle, label, and store in the refrigerator. Keeps for up to 3 months.

PISTACHIO ORGEAT

YIELD

About 1 L (34 fluid ounces)

INGREDIENTS

250 g (9 ounces) shelled pistachios

600 g (21 ounces) superfine sugar

600 ml (20 fluid ounces) hot water

3 ml (0.1 fluid ounce) orange flower water

30 ml (1 fluid ounce) Everclear or high-proof vodka

TOOLS

Induction cooktop, food processor, cheesecloth

METHOD

Place the pistachios in a medium size stainless-steel pot and add water to cover. Simmer at 60°C (140°F) for 30 minutes. Drain the pistachios, then transfer them to a food processor and process until smooth. Transfer to an airtight container, add the hot water to the pistachio paste and let sit for 2 hours. Strain through cheesecloth back into the pot and add the sugar and orange flower water. Cook at 70°C (158°F), stirring occasionally, until the sugar has completely dissolved. Remove from the heat, mix in the Everclear, and let cool to room temperature. Bottle, label, and store in the refrigerator. Keeps for up to 1 week.

RASPBERRY SYRUP

YIELD

About 1 L (34 fluid ounces)

INGREDIENTS

1 L (34 fluid ounces) semi-rich simple syrup (page 270)

170 g (6 ounces) raspberries

1 teaspoon rose water

7 ml (¼ ounce) Everclear or high-proof vodka

TOOLS

Vacuum bag, vacuum sealer, immersion circulator, water bath, cheesecloth

METHOD

Combine the syrup, raspberries, rose water, and Everclear in a vacuum bag. Vacuum-seal and sous-vide in a water bath at 45°C (113°F) for 4 hours. Strain the contents of the bag through cheesecloth. Bottle, label, and store in the refrigerator. Keeps for up to 2 weeks.

RASPBERRY-INFUSED GREEN SPOT

YIELD

750 mL (25 fluid ounces)

INGREDIENTS

200 g (7 ounces) frozen raspberries

750 mL (25 fluid ounces) Green Spot single pot still Irish whiskey

TOOLS

Vacuum bag, vacuum sealer, immersion circulator, water bath, cheesecloth

METHOD

Place the raspberries in a vacuum bag and pour in the whiskey. Seal bag with a vacuum sealer and sous-vide at 65°C (149°F) for 4 hours. Strain contents through cheesecloth and return to the whiskey bottle. Label and store in the refrigerator for up to 3 months.

RHUBARB SYRUP

YIELD

About 1 L (34 fluid ounces)

INGREDIENTS

¼ ounce rhubarb extract (Amoretti)

1 L (34 fluid ounces) simple syrup (page 272)

TOOLS

¼-ounce jigger, large bowl

METHOD

Whisk together the rhubarb extract and simple syrup in a large bowl until thoroughly mixed. Bottle, label, and store in the refrigerator. Keeps for up to 2 weeks.

SALINE SOLUTION

YIELD

About 945 ml (32 fluid ounces)

INGREDIENTS

100 grams (3.5 ounces) kosher salt

885 ml (30 fluid ounces) water

TOOLS

Scale

METHOD

Combine the salt and water in an airtight container, seal the lid, and shake until the salt has completely dissolved. Bottle, label, and store at room temperature. Keeps for up to 2 weeks.

SARSAPARILLA TINCTURE

YIELD

210 ml (about 7 fluid ounces)

INGREDIENTS

60 ml (2 fluid ounces) sarsaparilla extract

150 ml (5 fluid ounces) Everclear or high-proof vodka

METHOD

Combine the sarsaparilla extract and Everclear in an airtight container, seal the lid, and shake well. Bottle, label, and store at room temperature. Keeps for up to 3 months.

SEMI-RICH SIMPLE SYRUP

YIELD

600 ml (20 fluid ounces)

INGREDIENTS

800 g (28 ounces) superfine sugar

600 ml (20 fluid ounces) hot water

TOOLS

Scale, large bowl

METHOD

Whisk together the sugar and water in a large bowl until the sugar has completely dissolved. Bottle, label, and store in the refrigerator. Keeps for up to 2 weeks.

SESAME-INFUSED IRISH WHISKEY

YIELD

1 L (34 fluid ounces)

INGREDIENTS

1 tablespoon white sesame seeds

1 (750 ml/25 fluid ounces) bottle Irish whiskey (Powers Gold Label, Teeling Small Batch, or Kilbeggan)

TOOLS

Sauté pan

METHOD

Lightly toast the sesame seeds in a sauté pan over medium heat. While still hot, combine the toasted sesame seeds with the whiskey in a non-reactive airtight container. Let sit for 10 minutes, stirring often. Strain through a fine-mesh strainer. Bottle, label, and store at room temperature. Keeps for up to 3 months.

SHISO SYRUP

YIELD

355 ml (12 fluid ounces)

INGREDIENTS

700 g (25 ounces) superfine sugar

355 ml (12 fluid ounces) water

8 ounces shiso leaves

TOOLS

Spider strainer, cheesecloth, blender

METHOD

Whisk together the sugar and water in a large bowl until the sugar has completely dissolved. Set aside. Bring water to a boil in a medium stainless steel pot. Meanwhile, put some ice cubes in a medium bowl and fill with water for an ice bath. Immerse the shiso leaves in the boiling water for 15 seconds. Remove from the water and immediately submerge in the ice bath for 1 minute. Remove from the ice bath, pat dry with paper towels. Blend the blanched shiso leaves and reserved syrup on high speed in a blender for 1 minute. Strain through cheesecloth. Bottle, label, and store in the refrigerator. Keeps for up to 2 weeks.

SHISO TINCTURE

YIELD

1 L (34 fluid ounces)

INGREDIENTS

12 shiso leaves

1 L (34 fluid ounces) Everclear

TOOLS

Strainer

METHOD

Blanch the shiso leaves, then macerate them in the Everclear for 24 hours. Strain out the leaves through a fine-mesh strainer. Bottle, label, and store the tincture at room temperature. Keeps for up to 3 months.

SIMPLE SYRUP

YIELD

750 ml (25 fluid ounces)

INGREDIENTS

750 ml (25 fluid ounces) superfine sugar

750 ml (25 fluid ounces) hot water

TOOLS

Large bowl

METHOD

Whisk together the sugar and water in a large bowl until the sugar has completely dissolved. Bottle, label, and store in the refrigerator. Keeps for up to 2 weeks.

SPICED GUINNESS SYRUP

YIELD

1 L (34 fluid ounces)

INGREDIENTS

10 green cardamom pods, crushed

30 allspice berries

20 whole cloves

30 g (1 ounce) cassia cinnamon bark

3 bay leaves

1 L (34 fluid ounces) Guinness stout

2 vanilla beans, split lengthwise and seeds scraped out, pods cut into fourths

500 g (17.5 ounces) superfine sugar

TOOLS

Spice grinder, induction cooktop, cheesecloth

METHOD

Pulse the cardamom in a spice grinder, then transfer to a medium sauté pan. Add the allspice, cloves, cassia bark, and bay leaves. Lightly toast over medium heat, shaking the pan, until fragrant. Add the spices, Guinness, and vanilla seeds and diced pods to a medium stainless steel pot and bring to a boil over high heat, stirring frequently. Reduce the heat to low and simmer until the mixture has reduced by one-third. Add the sugar and stir to dissolve. Strain through cheesecloth. Bottle, label, and store in the refrigerator. Keeps for up to 2 weeks.

SPICED PEAR SYRUP

YIELD

1 L (34 fluid ounces)

INGREDIENTS

1 L (34 fluid ounces) cane syrup (page 243)

1 ripe Bartlett pear, cored and chopped

7 g (0.25 ounces) cassia cinnamon bark

2 bay leaves

20 whole cloves

TOOLS

Vacuum bag, vacuum sealer, immersion circulator, water bath, cheesecloth

METHOD

Combine the cane syrup, pear, cassia bark, bay leaves, and cloves in a vacuum bag. Vacuum-seal and sous-vide in a water bath at 52°C (125.6°F) for 6 hours. Strain through cheesecloth. Bottle, label, and store in the refrigerator. Keeps for up to 2 weeks.

SPICED SYRUP

YIELD

1 L (34 fluid ounces)

INGREDIENTS

750 ml (25 fluid ounces) water

750 g (26 ounces) sugar

10 whole cloves

2 bay leaves

20 allspice berries

5 g (0.18 ounce) cassia cinnamon bark

1 vanilla bean, halved lengthwise and seeds scraped out, pod cut into fourths

TOOLS

Induction cooktop, cheesecloth

METHOD

Combine the water, sugar, cloves, bay leaves, allspice, cassia bark, and vanilla seeds and diced pods in a medium size stainless-steel pot and stir well to soften the sugar. Bring to a boil, stirring often, then reduce the heat to 50°C (122°F) and simmer for 30 minutes. Remove from the heat and let cool for 15 minutes. Strain through cheesecloth. Bottle, label, and store in the refrigerator. Keeps for up to 2 weeks.

STRAWBERRY SYRUP

YIELD

1 L (34 fluid ounces)

INGREDIENTS

170 g (6 ounces) frozen strawberries, thawed

1 L (34 fluid ounces) cane syrup (page 243)

TOOLS

Vacuum bag, vacuum sealer, immersion circulator, water bath

METHOD

Place the strawberries and cane syrup in a vacuum bag. Vacuum-seal the bag and sous-vide in a water bath at 52°C (125.6°F) for 4 hours. Strain the contents of the bag through a fine-mesh strainer. Bottle, label, and store in the refrigerator. Keeps for up to 2 weeks.

SUMAC SYRUP

YIELD

1 L (34 fluid ounces)

INGREDIENTS

2 tablespoons ground sumac

500 ml (17 fluid ounces) water

1 kg (35 ounces) sugar

TOOLS

Induction cooktop, cheesecloth

METHOD

Combine the water and sumac in a medium size stainless-steel pot and heat at 100°C (212°F) until it comes to a boil. Add the sugar and stir frequently until the sugar has completely dissolved. Strain through cheesecloth and let cool to room temperature. Bottle, label, and store in the refrigerator. Keeps for up to 2 weeks.

SUNFLOWER ORGEAT

YIELD

About 4 L (135 fluid ounces)

INGREDIENTS

1 kg (35 ounces) hulled sunflower seeds

2.4 L (80 fluid ounces) hot water

2.4 kg (85 ounces) superfine sugar

30 ml (1 fluid ounce) Everclear

TOOLS

1-ounce jigger, induction cooktop, food processor, cheesecloth

METHOD

Place the sunflower seeds in a medium size stainless-steel pot and add water to cover. Simmer at 60°C (140°F) for 30 minutes. Drain the sunflower seeds, then transfer them to a food processor and process until smooth. Transfer to an airtight container, add the hot water to the sunflower seed paste and let sit for 2 hours. Strain through cheesecloth back into the pot and add the sugar. Cook at 70°C (158°F), stirring occasionally, until the sugar has completely dissolved. Remove from the heat, add the Everclear, and let cool to room temperature. Bottle, label, and store in the refrigerator. Keeps for up to 2 weeks.

SWEET POTATO SYRUP

YIELD

1 L (34 fluid ounces)

INGREDIENTS

1 L (34 fluid ounces) water

300 g (7 ounces) sweet potato, peeled and shredded

750 g (26.5 ounces) superfine sugar

TOOLS

Cheesecloth

METHOD

Place the water and sweet potato in a medium size stainless-steel pot. Bring to a boil over high heat, then reduce heat to low and let simmer until the liquid has reduced by a quarter. Remove from heat and let cool at room temperature for about 30 minutes. Strain the mixture through a cheesecloth. Return the liquid to the pot, add the sugar, and cook at 70°C (158°F) stirring frequently, until the sugar is completely dissolved. Let cool to room temperature. Bottle, label, and store in the refrigerator. Keeps for up to 2 weeks.

TOASTED FENNEL SALT

YIELD

Yield varies

INGREDIENTS

Dried fennel seeds

Salt

TOOLS

Induction cooktop, scale, spice grinder

METHOD

Lightly toast dried fennel seeds over low heat, being careful not to burn them. Once fennel seeds are lightly browned, take off heat and let cool to room temperature. Weigh the seeds and then measure an equal amount of kosher salt. Take the fennel seeds only and put in a spice grinder to finely grind the fennel seeds. Mix the ground fennel and kosher salt and shake until evenly mixed. Keep in a sealed container. It will last as long as it stays dry and smells good—we recommend no longer than 6 months.

TONKA BEAN SYRUP

YIELD

1 L (34 fluid ounces)

INGREDIENTS

1 whole tonka bean

500 ml (17 fluid ounces) water

1 kg (35 ounces) superfine sugar

TOOLS

Plastic gloves, induction cooktop, cheesecloth

METHOD

Wearing gloves, split and gut the tonka bean, exposing the flesh, and put it in a medium size stainless-steel pot. Add the water and bring to a boil, add the sugar and return the mixture to a boil. Cook, stirring frequently, until the sugar has completely dissolved. Strain through cheesecloth into an airtight container and let cool to room temperature. Bottle, label, and store in the refrigerator. Keeps for up to 4 weeks.

TURMERIC CITRUS

YIELD

500 ml (17 fluid ounces)

INGREDIENTS

500 ml (17 fluid ounces) water

3 tablespoons ground turmeric

1 tablespoon citric acid

Zest of 1 lime

TOOLS

Citrus zester, induction cooktop, coffee filter

METHOD

Combine the water, turmeric, citric acid, and lime zest in a medium size stainless-steel pot and heat at 70°C (158°F) until the mixture comes to a simmer. Simmer for 10 minutes, stirring occasionally. Strain through a coffee filter. Bottle, label, and store in the refrigerator. Keeps for up to 2 weeks.

VANILLA SYRUP

YIELD

750 ml (25 fluid ounces)

INGREDIENTS

1 Tahitian vanilla bean, sliced lengthwise, scraped, pod cut into fourths

500 g (17.5 ounces) superfine sugar

500 ml (17 fluid ounces) water

TOOLS

Induction cooktop, cheesecloth

METHOD

Scrape the seeds from the vanilla bean into the pot, add the sugar, and mix. Add the water and simmer at 70°C (158°F), stirring occasionally, for 1 hour. Remove from the heat and let cool. Strain through cheesecloth. Bottle, label, and store in the refrigerator. Keeps for up to 2 weeks.

WALNUT ANGOSTURA BITTERS

YIELD

About 475 ml (16 fluid ounces)

INGREDIENTS

⅓ cup walnuts

1 (473 ml/16 fluid ounce) bottle Angostura bitters

TOOLS

Sauté pan, blender, cheesecloth

METHOD

Toast the walnuts lightly in a sauté pan over low heat. Transfer the nuts to a blender, add the bitters, and blend until smooth. Let sit for 5 minutes, then strain through a fine-mesh strainer lined with cheesecloth. Bottle, label, and store at room temperature. Keeps for up to 6 months.

WHITE CHOCOLATE– INFUSED PIERRE FERRAND 1840 COGNAC

YIELD

750 ml (25 fluid ounces)

INGREDIENTS

400 g (14 ounces) white chocolate chips

750 ml (25 fluid ounces) Pierre Ferrand 1840 Cognac

TOOLS

Vacuum bag, vacuum sealer, immersion circulator, water bath, cheesecloth

METHOD

Place the white chocolate in a vacuum bag and pour in the cognac. Vacuum-seal the bag and sous-vide in a water bath at 65°C (149°F) for 4 hours. Remove from the water bath and let cool for 1 hour, then place the bag in the freezer for 24 hours, or until the oil freezes. Strain the contents of the bag through cheesecloth. Bottle, label, and store in the refrigerator. Keeps for up to 3 months.

WHITE MISO CANE SYRUP

YIELD

1 L (34 fluid ounces)

INGREDIENTS

500 ml (17 fluid ounces) water

2 tablespoons white miso paste

1 kg (35 ounces) cane sugar

TOOLS

Induction cooktop

METHOD

Place the water and miso in a medium size stainless-steel pot and heat at 80°C (176°F), stirring frequently, until the miso has completely dissolved. Add the sugar and increase the temperature to 100°C (212°F). Bring to a boil, stirring occasionally. Remove from the heat and let cool for 30 minutes. Bottle, label, and refrigerate for up to 2 weeks.

ZA'ATAR TINCTURE

YIELD

1 L (34 fluid ounces)

INGREDIENTS

500 ml (17 fluid ounces) Everclear or high-proof vodka

¼ cup za'atar

500 ml (17 fluid ounces) water

TOOLS

Cheesecloth or coffee filter

METHOD

Mix the Everclear and za'atar in an airtight container and let sit at room temperature for 48 hours. Strain through cheesecloth or a coffee filter and whisk in the water. Bottle, label, and store at room temperature for up to 3 months.

GLOSSARY

Here are some key terms you may find useful in exploring the world of Irish whiskey.

ABV

This stands for Alcohol By Volume, a ratio indicating the strength or proof of the whiskey. By law, Irish whiskey must be a minimum of 40 percent ABV.

AGE STATEMENT

A number usually found on the label of a whiskey bottle. In the case of a blend, it indicates the youngest whiskey used in the production of the bottle's contents.

ANGELS' SHARE

The portion of whiskey lost to the ether during maturation. The name is whimsical, the pain of loss is real.

BLEND

Most Irish whiskey is a blend of pot still, grain, and/or single malt whiskey. This is where blending becomes an art form. Classics include Jameson, Tullamore D.E.W., Bushmills, and Powers.

BOURBON CASK

More accurately, this is an "ex-bourbon" cask—that is, it formerly contained ageing bourbon. It is many distillers' preferred type of cask for maturing Irish whiskey.

CASK STRENGTH

A number indicating that the whiskey was not diluted when it was taken from the barrel and bottled. This means it is higher proof—in other words, stronger.

CHILL FILTERING

An optional process at the bottling stage designed to prevent a whiskey from going cloudy.

COLOR

All whiskey is clear when it goes into the barrel for maturing. The type of wood used at this stage and at finishing will ultimately provide the color of the *uisce beatha* in your glass.

COLUMN STILL

The younger of the two main stills of the distillation world, having only been around for less than 200 years—the blink of an eye in whiskey time. It produces a lighter, purer grain spirit with a weaker flavor, but higher ABV.

CONDENSER

Part of the still that collects alcohol vapor driven off during distillation.

CONGENERS

Chemical compounds other than ethanol or water that come through the still and may contribute a distinctive character to the spirit.

COOPER

A skilled maker and repairer of barrels and casks. A hugely important figure in any distillery.

COOPERAGE

In the land of whiskey, this has two meanings. First, it is the making and maintaining of barrels and casks (precious assets for any distillery). Second, it refers to ageing of whiskey in barrels, since conventional wisdom says much of the final taste of a whiskey results from its cooperage.

DISTILLATION

This process through which grain, water, and yeast become Irish whiskey. See pages 35–36 for a detailed explanation of this particular alchemy.

DUNNAGE (SEE RACKHOUSE)

FEINTS

Also known as the tails, these are the last part of the distillate produced. They are oilier and less volatile than the heart and are usually siphoned off and redistilled with the heads.

FERMENTATION

The wort is cooled and poured into a fermentation vessel (also called a washback). These are usually stainless steel, though wooden ones are still in use. Yeast is then added, and things get going, as the sugars in the wort are converted into alcohol.

FINISH

A tasting term to describe what happens immediately after you've taken a sip of whiskey, as the flavors continue to develop on the palate.

FINISHING

After whiskey has matured for a number of years—usually in bourbon casks—it is often "finished" for a second, shorter period of time in a different type of cask. Barrels seasoned by previously containing fortified wines—sherry, port, Madeira, etc.—are popular, though distillers will often experiment with other types, such as rum and cognac, or, Chardonnay, Merlot, and Bordeaux wine barrels. Finishing delivers depth of flavor, and profoundly influences the aroma and color of the whiskey.

FILL (FIRST, SECOND)

A cask in which, for example, sherry, port, bourbon, or other spirits were matured is known as a "first fill." These are preferred for maturing whiskey. Second- and even third-fill casks are also used, but the influence of the original spirit on the whiskey declines markedly each time.

GRAIN TO GLASS

This term describes a whiskey that has been produced using the distiller's own barley and own new-make spirit (see Sourced Whiskey). The entire process is controlled by the distiller. Clonakilty and Echlinville are good examples. Sometimes also called "farm to glass" or "field to glass."

GRIST (SEE MILLING)

HEADS

These are the earliest evaporations from the distillation process. They contain less-desirable compounds, which the distiller identifies using the spirit safe. The heads are usually discarded, but sometimes they are redistilled with the feints or tails.

HEART

The middle section of the distillation sandwich—the good stuff, with none of the early unpleasant elements ("heads") or the later unpleasant ones ("tails").

LAUTER TUN

A type of mash filter, sometimes also called a mash tun. It works much like a large sieve to separate solids from the mash.

LOW WINES

The product of the first distillation in a pot still.

MALT

Barley that has sprouted—thereby making its stored starch available as fermentable sugars.

MALTING

The process of tricking the barley into germinating, which triggers the production of enzymes. These in turn will convert the starch into the sugars needed by yeast for distillation.

MASHBILL

The mixture of various grains used to make the wort.

MASHING

Here, the grist is mixed with warm water in a mash tun. This triggers the conversion of starch to sugars, ready for exposure to yeast. The process is repeated two more times.

MASH FILTER

A technology that separates the sugar solution from the malt solids. This is more traditional in brewing than distilling. Midleton has one of these. Many distillers use the Lauter tun instead.

MASH TUN (SEE LAUTER TUN)

MILLING

The process in which the malt is ground into a coarse flour-like material called grist.

NEW-MAKE

Newly made spirit.

OAK

This is the standard wood used for whiskey barrels. Almost all Irish whiskey matures in oak before being finished in another type of wood. Broadly speaking, there are two species of oak involved, American and European. The former is used exclusively in bourbon-making, and ex-bourbon casks are greatly favored for whiskey. European oak tends to be used in first-fill wine-making, and so features in distilling for secondary distilling or finishing.

PEATED

A style of whiskey more associated with Scotch. It is made with barley that has been peat-dried, which lends a distinctive smoky note. The most popular Irish peated whiskey is Kilbeggan's Connemara, though some of the new generation of distillers are also experimenting with the style.

POITÍN

Sometimes spelled potcheen or poteen and pronounced put-CHEEN, it is the clear and ancient spirit—Irish moonshine. Many distilleries now produce it commercially and, yes, legally.

PORT PIPE

The distinctive type of barrel in which port is matured. Some whiskey distillers use these for secondary finishing.

POT ALE

This is the liquor left in the wash still after the first distillation. It is protein-rich and distilleries often pass it on to local farmers for use in animal feed (along with the dry residue called draff).

POT STILL

The oldest form of still used in Irish whiskey-making. It has a distinctive bulb or dome shape that goes back to the alembics that monks first used to distill medicine and fragrances in the medieval era. The term is also used to describe the superior traditional style of malt whiskey that the still produces.

RACKHOUSE

In a rackhouse, whiskey barrels were traditionally stored on their sides, rather than upright. Some distillers maintain that this gives more contact between the whiskey and the seasoned cask wood, and that this helps develop flavor.

RECTIFICATION

The process of purifying or refining a spirit by repeated or continuous distillation.

REFLUX

A process by which alcohol vapors are condensed and returned to the distillation chamber in order to purify them.

SHERRY BUTT

Type of cask often used for finishing an aged whiskey. The fortified wine residue absorbed in the wood lends color and flavor.

SINGLE GRAIN

An Irish whiskey from one distillery. Can be produced using corn, wheat, or barley—with a small addition of malted barley for those useful enzymes. Typically made in a column still.

SINGLE MALT

An Irish whiskey made using only malted barley.

SINGLE POT STILL

A style of whiskey that can only be legally made in Ireland. It is produced in a pot still at a single distillery using both malted and unmalted barley.

SOURCED WHISKEY

Many distilleries will contract the supply of a particular style of distillate that they do not produce themselves from another distiller—for use in, say, a blend. This is known as sourced whiskey. For example, Cooley and Midleton supply much of the sourced grain whiskey produced in Ireland today.

SPIRIT SAFE

This is a large, glass-walled box that sits within the distillation chain. It's crucial for allowing the distiller to assess the spirit coming out of the pot still, and deciding when to stop (or "cut") distillation.

STILL

This is the heart of the distillery, the apparatus in which the magic happens. There are two types used in whiskey-making: the pot still and the column still. The latter is sometimes called the Coffey still, after its inventor, Aeneas Coffey.

TAILS

These are the later evaporations from the distillation process. They contain fewer desirable compounds, so the distiller will want to identify these in the spirit safe and either discard them or redistill them with the heads.

UISCE BEATHA

The original Irish term that eventually became anglicized into "whiskey." It's pronounced ISH-ka BAH-ha and means "the water of life."

VATTING

In the past, vatting was synonymous with blending. Today though, there's a distinction. When a single distillery combines multiple barrels of their whiskey in order to achieve a consistent flavor profile, this is vatting. Blending involves mixing whiskey from different distilleries.

WAREHOUSE

More than just a storage facility, the warehouse is actually a crucial component in the whiskey ageing process. Here, the whiskey is in prolonged contact with the cask wood. Air is moving around the casks. (Some coastal distillers insist that the sea air definitely affects the flavor of their whiskey.) The whiskey casks are either palletized and vertically stacked or laid horizontally on their sides. In the latter case the warehouse is called a rackhouse, rickhouse, or dunnage.

WHISKEY

A spirit distilled in Ireland from grain (usually barley), yeast, and water and matured for at least four years. A miracle.

WORT

This is the liquid produced by mashing malted barley. It contains all the sugars that the yeast will convert to alcohol.

INDEX

Note: Entries in green refer to cocktail recipe names.

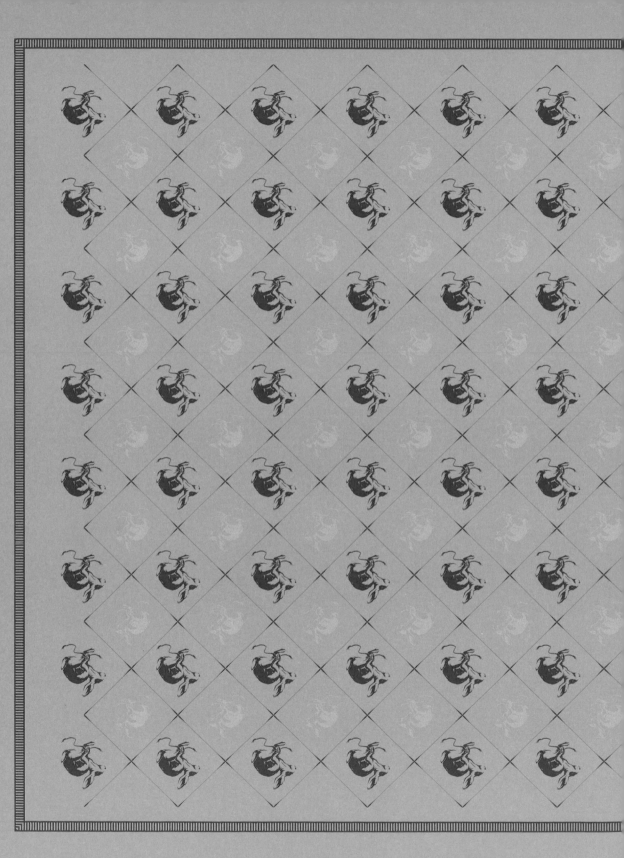